BEREAV

Bereaved

IAN KNOX

KINGSWAY PUBLICATIONS
EASTBOURNE

ISBN 0 85476 379 1

Produced by Bookprint Creative Services
P.O. Box 827, BN21 3YJ, England for
KINGSWAY PUBLICATIONS LTD
Lottbridge Drove, Eastbourne, E Sussex BN23 6NT.
Printed in Great Britain

For Dad, Mum, Keith, Sue and Martin

Contents

Foreword

When Ian first told me that he wanted to write a book about bereavement, I encouraged him. I think I did so as a friend and because I sensed that there was something unusually deep within him that lay behind what he wanted to do.

I hope he will forgive me if I say that I never realised he would write such a good and moving book! For me, Ian is a courageous and energetic evangelist. He drives himself hard and displays a powerful commitment to the gospel. What this book reveals is that Ian is also an intensely human and sensitive person. More than that, he is someone ready to do a great deal of homework to collect stories of real people facing a wide range of painful situations. This is a book about many types of bereavement. Ian's way of looking at different sorts of loss and seeing them also as bereavements is another of the surprises of the book. But it is a good surprise!

To read this book is to become more human. I found myself with a lump in my throat again and again as I read through it. Death is a subject that our society finds very hard to cope with. As a result, we avoid discussing it and, as a further result, we are often very weak at comforting the dying and supporting the bereaved.

I think this book will be a great help to many of us. It is full of hope, but it is also honest about suffering and sorrow. Ian shows that he is an evangelist who does *not* come up with glib and unrealistic answers. I am glad I read it. I warmly commend it.

+ *Gavin Maidstone*

Introduction
Start Here

Bereavement is like a maze. The twists and turns and cul-de-sacs can drive us to despair. We wonder which way to go. Is there any way out? Does anyone have any pointers as to the direction we might take? So often the feeling is of being lost, and of being helpless and hopeless. The good news is that there is a way through, though it may be long and painful. And, in the end, there is a way out.

This may be a hard book to read. It is a tough subject. Indeed, I did not realise how hard until I came to deal with it and to talk with many people who had been bereaved in one way or another. The very word 'bereaved' is strongly emotive. The Chambers English Dictionary has this definition: 'Bereave – to rob of anything valued: to deprive: to widow, orphan, or deprive by death of some dear relative or friend: to snatch away.' It then shows how the word comes from the Old English 'bereafian', meaning 'to plunder'. This is strong talk, and yet we will see it is correct. Bereavement is very often a great deal more than just 'goodbye'. It is at least an unwelcome loss of someone or something that is precious and, at its worst, a robbery of that which is the most important thing in a person's life.

Of course, no one will identify personally with every bereavement described in this book, but we will see how others have been hurt and how they have learned to cope. As a result, their experiences may help us with our different loss, and their way to relief may help us. Thus, if a particular passage from the Bible has helped someone in a special need, that passage may also fit your situation.

But there is another kind of reader this book is intended for, a much wider grouping, and that is those of us who know someone who is grieving a loss. What are they going through, and how can I help – or hinder – that process?

This is a book which displays a lot of hurts. Some of those hurts have been healed, or are on the way to a healing. But some bereavements will be shown as not having found a solution, as yet. One thing I have tried to show is that grieving is right: it could be dangerous not to grieve. But I am also aiming to encourage, knowing that God cares, and he will help. It was Jesus Christ himself who said, 'Blessed are those who mourn, for they will be comforted' (Matthew 5:4).

Bereavement is a mixture of triumph and tragedy, hope and despair, joy and sorrow. This difficult and delicate balance is never more remarkably demonstrated than in an incident in the life of Jesus Christ. A friend of his, called Lazarus, had died. When Jesus arrived at the home of Lazarus, one of the dead man's sisters, Martha, went out to meet Jesus. 'If you had been here, my brother would not have died,' she reprimands him. In no way offended, Jesus offers Martha words of hope which are so special that we still use them at the beginning of many a funeral service: 'I am the resurrection and the life. He who believes in me will live, even though he dies; and whoever lives and believes in me will never die.' There were never spoken such words of assurance and hope. So what does Jesus do next? This whole incident, in John 11, is famous for containing the shortest verse in the Bible,

John 11:35: 'Jesus wept.' He has just spoken with such triumph, and then immediately shares so completely in the tragedy that he sheds tears of grief.

The experts tell us that the grief which follows bereavement has various stages to it. The steps, we are told, go like this: denial, shock, numbness, emptiness, anger, grief, depression and, finally, acceptance. I am not an expert, nor am I going to pretend I have become one by writing this book. If you want to go deeper into this whole subject you will need to read the classic by Colin Murray-Parkes, *Bereavement – Studies of Grief in Adult Life*, published by Penguin, which includes an extensive bibliography. Compared with Murray-Parkes this is very much a personal book and I have written from experience – my own and others'. I would agree with the experts that these stages of grief do happen. However, they do not all happen for everyone, and they rarely occur in such a neat order. The phases often recur, and can easily take place out of sequence. For each person, the grief pattern is always unique. Each person's bereavement will find echoes in that of others, but it will always be individual in some of its aspects.

I have tried to be extremely honest, and I am not going to give pat or clinchéd answers. We should not be surprised when reading of the lady who wants to spit at well-meaning comforters, or of the Christian leader who still cannot hold back the tears nearly twenty years after his baby has died. This is no theoretical treatise. This is where the action is! We will meet people who are angry, and others who have got stuck at one of the steps in grieving and have been unable to move on.

But we will also find that Jesus Christ is able to bring hope, even at the darkest moment. I find great help from a particularly poignant incident in Luke 24. Two of Jesus' disciples are walking to their home in Emmaus, a village near Jerusalem, on the Sunday evening after Jesus has been killed on the cross the previous Friday. As they travel with 'their faces downcast', Luke tells us that 'Jesus himself came up and walked along with them' (Luke 24:15). So while reading this book, let's allow Jesus to walk with us. In every chapter there is help from the Bible, God's word to us. (My abbreviation 'Luke 24:15' means the verse is in the Gospel of Luke, chapter 24, verse 15.)

I have divided the book into two main sections. The first eight chapters deal with different bereavements where there has been an actual physical death. This is 'the long goodbye'. If a partner has died, I have dealt with that loss in four chapters, namely 1, 2, 5 and 6. Chapters 9–16 deal with bereavement through life: something has happened to deprive us of a special aspect of our life – a child has left home, a divorce has occurred, illness has meant a curtailment of activity, and so on. In every case there is a sense of real loss, and the grief this causes. I actually came to write this because of a 'bereavement through life' of my own. Chapter 9 will explain this! We never know when a day will change our lives.

Whatever our situation, we should remember that God does care. Friends, ministers and counsellors will listen, and can give help and support. Above all, let's not despair.

> May the God of peace, who through the blood of the eternal covenant brought back from the dead our Lord Jesus, that great Shepherd of the sheep, equip you with everything good for doing his will, and may he work in us what is pleasing to him, through Jesus Christ, to whom be glory for ever and ever. Amen (Hebrews 13:20–21).

Thank you to the scores of people who have allowed me

to tell their stories. I hope the kaleidoscope of characters does not confuse anyone, but I felt that each new person was able to add their own unique contribution. In most cases, even their names are correct, as is every detail of the narrative. For obvious reasons one or two names have been changed (their names are in 'inverted commas'), but the stories are still absolutely true.

Thank you to the Director of the 40:3 Trust, Brian Camfield and his wife Christine, and to my sister, Sue Crookes, for their advice on the draft of the book. I'm so grateful to my long-time friend, Gavin Reid, for his generous foreword. Thank you to my family for letting me share their lives. Maria and Yvonne in my office have worked hard, and I give a big kiss to my wife, Ruth, for doing all the typing, and for keeping me going through this amazing adventure. My life has been enriched and deepened by the courage of others, and by the love of God revealed in suffering. I pray that others, too, will let God bless them as they read.

Ian Knox

PART ONE

Bereaved by Death

1

Nearest and Dearest: a Parent

'Mother's dead.'

My dad was on the telephone. I was just back at my 'digs' in the South of England after a morning at the College of Law, studying for my finals to qualify as a solicitor. I had no idea Gran was ill, but she was reasonably old, and I was sorry for Dad that his mother would no longer be with us. I tried to tell him how sorry I was, and that we would miss her.

'No, not my mother – your mother. Mum. She died this morning.'

6.6.66 is an easy date for anyone to remember. But when it is the day on which your mother died at the age of forty-five, with no warning that this was even remotely possible, you remember without a doubt. A phone call like that changes your life. You are never the same person again. The death of your parent is, in a moment, the end of part of your life and, at the same time, the beginning of a new life. How you view it depends a great deal on where your life is at the time. I have asked three or four people to tell me how they reacted to Mum's death, but first here's how I remember it.

To say I was shocked understates my feelings by a long way. My mind had been blinkered with the most vital exams of my life about to happen. I had just returned from my family home in Yorkshire after a half-term break, saying goodbye to a perfectly fit mother on her way to watch *The Sound of Music*. Now, four days later, I was struggling with my worst subject, trying to cram 'Book-keeping and Trust Accounts' into my non-mathematical brain. Little did I know what 'struggling' really was – till Dad's message.

A quick call to the college, a hasty note to my landlady, a few things shoved into a bag and I was dashing for a train. Numbed with horror, the journey was a blur. Some poor woman, sitting opposite me on the long ride North, got the brunt of my pain, as I talked on and on about this mother of mine. Maybe God put some sort of angel in that seat because, whoever she was, she seemed to listen with real kindness and understanding. In most of the subsequent interviews I have done for this book, I have found how important it is to have a kind listener, who will allow a shocked, recently bereaved person to pour out their loss and verbalise their hurt.

At home, Dad and I held each other, two men without the most important woman in their lives. The first day or so was taken up with necessary activity – collecting the death certificate, arranging the funeral, sorting out some of the things we had taken for granted because 'Mum does that'.

It was only on the third morning that I was amazed by something I should have expected. I was alone in the house when the post arrived. There were dozens of letters and cards – part of over 400 in all from friends and family – and I started to open them. One of them said something or other which seemed to sum up my own love for Mum, and I fell apart. I started to carry the letter upstairs, but found I could not walk, so I simply lay face down on the stairs and wept my heart out. I seemed to cry for ever, till I had no tears left.

I remember two things especially about that weeping time. The first was that I asked God, 'Why? Why has my mum died? Why has this happened now? What are we going to do?' And I heard, quite distinctly, God's answer. It was such an odd answer, I could not have made it up, because God said, very clearly, 'Ask me that in five years.' And the funny thing was, it seemed a perfectly reasonable reply! Even in my sobbing, I could see that I was totally unable to take in any logical reasoning, and I would need time to adjust to enable me to understand.

Lying on the stairs, I was comforted by what God would show me – and I was then given a great sense of reassurance. I knew that the Bible said, 'The eternal God is your refuge, and underneath are the everlasting arms' (Deuteronomy 33:27). That morning, I experienced what those words meant. And this is the second thing I remember especially. I felt as if I were falling through space, and my tears would kill me. And then I felt strong arms catch me, very gently, and hold me safe. I was so distraught, I could not have conjured up such a sensation, but it was very real, and all these years later I can still feel God's loving grip around me then, and the deep peace that came into my broken heart. I have shed tears over Mum's death since, but they have never been tears of hopelessness: God's love and care and understanding are not just things preachers talk about; they are realities God gives.

So when, at the funeral, we sang:

> Jesus lives, thy terrors now
> Can, O death, no more appal us

I knew all was well. My mum had trusted Jesus as her Saviour twenty-one years before. She had lived as a lovely Christian, and it was she who had helped me entrust my own life to Christ when I was a boy. Now she knew for herself the victory Jesus had won over death.

After a week it was back to college, and work proved an excellent antidote to moping around. And I did pass all the exams to qualify as a solicitor. Life was different, but not as bad as I had feared. Perhaps part of the reason was that I had left home some months before, and my daily contact with Mum had already been broken. For those living at home, it must have been worse. My sister Sue was fifteen when Mum died, and the only girl among three brothers. For her, grief was harder – and came later.

On the night Mum was rushed to hospital by ambulance, Sue was led to believe it was a stomach upset – the things we tell children! So to this day Sue regrets not saying 'goodbye'. The next morning she was packed off to school and, not knowing anything untoward was happening, she dilly-dallied on her way home, only to find Dad's car in the drive. Her main concern was thinking up an excuse for being late (walking home with boys was the real reason!), but the question never arose. For there was Dad, standing by the sink, saying, 'I've got something very sad to tell you,' and bursting into floods of tears. 'Your mum died in hospital.'

You do odd things when a special person dies. My sister blurted out, 'I must tell Sue' (her best friend), grabbed an apple, and ran half a mile to Sue's house where she knocked on the door and almost fell in, crying the news to Sue's mother. The next day she went to school and feels, on reflection, it would have been better not to. A friend asked her, 'What are you looking so miserable about?' and was devastated at Sue's news. The only day she took off school was for the funeral. And the only time she really cried was when our ten-year-old brother Martin hugged his teddy and asked, 'What have I done wrong?

Why wasn't it Christopher's mummy?' (Christopher was the naughtiest boy in his school.)

Walking behind the coffin with everybody looking was dreadful for Sue. Not being allowed to go to the graveside is also a regret. But she does not remember grieving, mainly because she took on the role of being Mother. So her memories are of things like putting a hot iron through a headscarf and a petticoat, and of putting fish and chips in the oven with the paper still round them and burning the paper. She never thought there was anything else for it but to act as Mum. Life became very restricted and, as no one ever talked about Mum, life just went on, with an implicit denial that a death had ever happened.

Unlike my experience, Sue was not conscious of God's help, though she found that Christians were kind, and God comforted her through them. Her grief sat in limbo for ten years, till our brother Keith died – the brother between her and me in age. With two bereavements needing to be dealt with, Sue then went for counselling for a year at the doctors' surgery where she worked. Now a counsellor herself, she still finds it hard when helping someone with a similar story to hers. But she has now known God's healing. Like any woman, she misses her mum most strongly when there are good things to share.

And what of the grief of a ten-year-old, when his mum dies? Of course my younger brother Martin had no inkling that Mum was ill, let alone dying. He knew she had been taken into hospital, but had no suspicion it was serious. It was half-term for his junior school, so Dad took him to the hospital. He understands now why he was not allowed to see her, looking so ill, but is sorry he did not. He was taken to Dad's office, and sat alone in Dad's big chair till Dad came back, burst into tears and said, 'Mummy's dead.' Martin had never seen Dad cry before, and they sat and cried together: a very positive experience for Martin. This holding and cuddling was very important to Martin, and should be remembered for children in grief.

A good friend took Sue and Martin to stay at her house that night, and Martin especially remembers the pink and white striped sheets, and the physical comfort from both the friend and Sue.

Martin is glad he went to the funeral, and remembers singing:

> How sweet the name of Jesus sounds
> In a believer's ear.
> It soothes his sorrows, heals his wounds,
> And drives away his fear.

But, unlike Sue, he is glad he did not go to the graveside. From the experience of Sue and Martin, it seems that children can handle what they know, rather than what they do not know. Telling them is better than not doing so. They should be offered the opportunity to go to the funeral, and at least be offered the chance of going to the graveside. Children do grieve, and should be encouraged to do so – but only if they want to.

In particular, children need support. Martin is glad there was a full, caring church for the funeral. He felt buoyed up, as if he actually were a buoy in a sea of kind friends, amounting to a physical feeling. When Dad said he felt supported by people's prayers, Martin identified with that, even at the age of ten. But with that mature approach there were also the childish concerns. He felt at the time he was somehow responsible for her death, though now conceding how totally irrational this was! The previous evening he had asked Mum to play football with him, to which she had replied, 'I'll play with you tomorrow.' He had then thrown a rugby ball, which had accidentally hit her in the back. For the next five years he was convinced he had caused her death, and never told anyone. In the end he realised how silly this was. Children's fears need to be expressed – and allayed.

Having said that, Martin was able to approach Mum's death reasonably positively. At the time he was able to cry a lot, and was consoled by Sue. The crying soon stopped, and was out of his system. He was given time to grieve: he never felt anyone stopped him, and he was allowed to be himself. He never felt bitter, nor that Mum's death was unfair. It was only when he was nineteen that he was able to articulate this, when a friend asked him, 'Have you ever felt bitter towards God at losing your mother?' to which he simply replied, 'Some people die at forty-five.' His regret at Mum's not being alive now is because his children have never seen her – but he has come through well.

I also found that, as time passed, my questions were answered, as I understood the more positive side of Mum's death. I discovered what bereavement was, and was able to come alongside others in similar circumstances whom I would never have been able to help if I had not suffered myself. I was able to prove God's power in my life, healing my grief, in a way I had not known previously. I saw how God sharpened the lives of each member of my family, giving a cutting edge to our Christianity.

But suppose we had all been that little bit older, married and away from home, and Mum had died suddenly: would we have coped better? The answer is almost certainly 'no'. I have a friend called 'Mary'. Mary's parents, and one of her brothers, were killed in a horrendous car crash which burned all three to death. Mary was married with two small children, and had thus not lived with her parents, or even near them, for years. Their deaths were nevertheless life-shattering for her. For a long time she refused even to hear what had happened in the accident, especially when she received a manilla envelope from the police containing her mother's gold wedding ring. This had been the only means of identification.

I think that type of grief may actually be worse the older you are. Mary's feeling was initially numbness. Her whole body went cold, and she spent hours in a hot bath trying to get warm. She sobbed so much she was constantly thirsty. For two days she ate nothing, till a friend arrived with a casserole for the family. Practical help can be of great value. Mary ached through each day and wept through each night. Phoning people to let them know was agony. Mary hated to hurt those who had loved her parents so much. That Sunday at church the entire congregation wept.

But Mary soon realised there were two sorts of people. First, there were those who had been in a similar situation themselves, and knew what to say: some near neighbours were brilliant because they had also lost a parent in a car crash. Because of their experience of sudden loss and grief, they were not scared off by Mary's tragedy. Then there were those who could not cope with Mary and her family being there, because they had not 'been there' themselves. Those people needed Mary to approach them, not vice versa, and they included mature Christians. They would often deliberately avoid Mary: it was too painful and awkward.

One of Mary's hardest problems was explaining things to her three-year-old son, who would not accept the permanent separation from his grandparents. In the bath, her son picked up the soap Granny had given him and said, 'I don't think I thanked her. I'll write to her and post it to heaven. No, I'll phone her up.' Mary's temptation was to be over-kind and give in to her son's fantasy.

In the end she was saved by a pet guinea pig, which died some time later, and enabled the son to grieve for it, and for his grandparents.

And Mary herself slowly got over her loss. Through the first year she felt God so close he could be touched, and in the second year she felt her grieving was complete, though some sorrow still remains.

But my ultimate question was not, 'How would I have coped if I'd been older?' but rather, 'How did my dad survive Mum's death?' The other day I asked him. His first problem was the suddenness of it. He and Mum always went to bed wrapped in each other's arms, and that midnight Mum had complained of a great pain in her chest. 'What's it like to have a heart attack?' she asked, immediately adding, 'I'm dying.' In the next breath she went on, 'How ever will you manage with all those children? See my mother and brother and talk to them. Tell my girls to be in time.' When you are married you learn verbal shorthand. My mother was concerned to be sure her own mother and brother were Christians – which they subsequently became – and she wanted the girls in her Bible class to be Christians too. After her death, Dad carried out all her requests.

At the time he only had one thing in mind – Mum's survival. Having no phone, he rushed round the corner to fetch a specialist who lived in the next street, who sent Mum to hospital with the assurance that it was 'only indigestion'. By 10.30am she had suffered another heart attack, and was dead.

I don't think I know of a more touching relationship than that shared by my parents. They started courting when she was fourteen and he was twenty. Married at the beginning of World War Two, they wrote to each other for four-and-a-half years every day, twenty or thirty pages at a time, only seeing each other every six months. Those wartime letters proved a comfort during the months after Mum died. Dad never felt bitter, but was deeply lonely and sad. The great triangle of God, Mum and Dad seems not to have been broken. He still feels her near him, conscious of a oneness with her and God.

A few years later, Dad remarried, and has known much happiness with his second wife. But he still dreams about my mother and misses her as much now as on the day she died. He has never got over it. His memories are all happy, and he smilingly acknowledges that Mum would have hated growing old, losing her teeth, and having her beautiful raven-black hair turn white. Dad does not blame God, and though he would sometimes say as the psalmist does, 'Why are you downcast, O my soul? Why so disturbed within me?' he would also say, 'Put your hope in God, for I will yet praise him, my Saviour and my God' (Psalm 42:5).

Tennyson got it right when he wrote:

> And the stately ships go on
> To their haven under the hill;
> But O for the touch of a vanished hand
> And the sound of a voice that is still.

Viscount Hailsham, the former Lord Chancellor, was interviewed on BBC Radio 4 about the death of his first wife. 'The pain of parting is the price you pay for love. The greater the love, the greater the pain. I don't think there is any consolation.' Asked about his Christian faith, he replied, 'Faith is not a pain-killer. You feel as much pain believing or not believing. The cross was administered without an anaesthetic.'

But, and it is a big but, Lord Hailsham also said, 'I believe in the communion of saints – there would be no justice if she were not happy where she is.' And I agree!

Jesus said of his Father, 'He is not the God of the dead but of the living' (Matthew 22:32), when referring to Abraham, Isaac and Jacob who were long since dead, and yet alive in God's eternal kingdom. My mother is with Jesus Christ. Unfortunately, we are still here – it's the temporary separation that hurts! All these years later, the whole family thanks God for such a mum, such a wife.

2

It's Time to Go: the Elderly

The Frenchman who used to 'thank Heaven for little girls' – Maurice Chevalier – once said, 'Old age isn't so bad when you consider the alternative.' Unfortunately for him, he did have to 'consider the alternative' in the end. Because, in the end, we all die. This is not to be morbid, but the death rate is 100%. If we are not dead before we grow old, we will die when we are old.

Of course, few admit to being old. I was talking with my gran when she was ninety-eight – 'You know, Ian, there are some old people in our church.' She said it in a rather pitying way, and it was quite clear she did not include herself in their number. I wanted to look round her church and see these folk who topped ninety-eight years old. However, despite her implied denial, my gran *was* old, and death was to meet her three years later.

It was her husband, my grandfather, whose death was the first I remember. At the age of five I first learned that there is 'a time to be born and a time to die' (Ecclesiastes 3:2). Grandpa was my friend. As a small boy, I did not realise how ill he was, only that he would sit in a big round bay window in his bedroom. His home overlooked the sea at beautiful Cayton Bay, near Scarborough in Yorkshire, and he and I would spend what seemed to be endless hours being together when I visited him on holiday. I remember the quiet, and his kindness, and I never even noticed his shaking as Parkinson's disease caused his slow and final deterioration.

Back home, one morning, my mother came to my bedroom to wake me for school. 'We'll let Daddy lie in this morning,' she whispered. 'He's very sad: Grandpa has died.' I was sorry for Dad, but I wasn't sad myself. I could only think of Grandpa with happiness and, as he was old, naturally he had to die. Now I am older, I realise that to die in your mid-sixties is not so old after all, but it did not seem that way then. It helps me to put into perspective how a child reacts to death, and how he or she can cope much better than an adult. If I had been able to put my feelings into clever words as a five-year-old, I know what I felt was, 'Death has been swallowed up in victory. Where, O death, is your victory? Where, O death, is your sting? . . . But thanks be to God! He gives us the victory through our Lord Jesus Christ' (1 Corinthians 15:54–55, 57). Grandpa had gone to be with Jesus – it was all right.

I still think that reaction was right. But now I would temper it somewhat, as I realise that others face the death of someone who is older from different standpoints. What must my gran have felt? She did not realise it, but she was facing forty years as a widow, even though she had been married to Grandpa for forty years by the time he died. As Gran is now dead herself, I asked a friend of mine, Dorothy, how the partner left behind feels.

Dorothy and Norman were married for fifty-four years. Norman was my gardening adviser: what he didn't know about fruit and vegetables and flowers wasn't worth knowing. He sang in our church choir, and was the most positive of men. He radiated his love for God, and was one of my greatest encouragers for the Christian work I was doing. But Norman had cancer of the lymph glands, and he and Dorothy faced squarely the fact that he was dying. They talked about their being physically separated, and prepared for his death. After a period of hospitalisation, Norman came home as the end drew near. For the last three weeks, many of his friends came to say their goodbyes. 'It's done us good to see him,' they would say as they left, having experienced his shining faith in the Lord Jesus.

Quietly, one night, his body gave up the struggle. The funeral had tears, but much rejoicing, as all our memories were happy. But what of Dorothy? 'I knew it would happen,' she told me. 'It was easier than if it had been sudden, as there was no sense of shock. I was sad, but it wasn't overwhelming, and I mustn't let it be. Norman always said, "Keep bright!" and I wouldn't dare do any other! He wouldn't have wanted a lot of tears.' Dorothy still lives in the same house, sharing her home with a long-time friend, Muriel, which means she is not alone.

'I never think, "I'm a widow,"' Dorothy says. 'I know I am – it just seems funny to call myself that. I have my daughter and her husband and two granddaughters – they keep me young. So much reminds me of Norman – the garden, music – and I feel sad. Then I say, "You mustn't be like that." As I look back, all my memories are happy, and so I am able to look forward.'

Dorothy's main feeling is not of grief, but of gratitude. She is grateful for good friends, for those who cared for Norman in his illness, for the support of the church, and especially for a sense of well-being that all is well with her husband. He was so sure of his faith, and so certain of his heavenly destination, that Dorothy's sadness is never overwhelming. For the partner of an older person, bereavement is bound to be extremely painful, but need not be impossible to bear.

Other relatives may find that this approach can help them too. Peter is a friend of mine who knew for some time that his mother was fading. Like Norman, Peter's mother was nearly eighty. She was, said Peter, wearing out.

Unfortunately, Peter's early relationship with his mother had not been the best. Brought up in Ceylon (now Sri Lanka) where his father was a tea planter, Peter saw his mother for a couple of hours a day by appointment: those were the days of colonialism and nannies! Time away at boarding school, and then his parents' divorce and his mother's remarriage, further estranged them. When Peter returned to live in England with his wife, Jennifer, his mother, who had in the meantime moved to New Zealand, fell ill.

Adversity, treated positively, can lead to a fresh beginning, and so it proved in this family. Peter and Jennifer moved his mother to England, where they could care for her near their home. Slowly, the old barriers came down. A large part of the secret behind this was Peter's Christian commitment, and the friendship his church friends showed to this lady who knew no one. The greatest moment of all was when, at the age of seventy-four, Peter's mother attended a church service. When an invitation was given for people to entrust their lives to the Lord Jesus Christ, she went forward to the front of the church to acknowledge publicly her new faith. Peter had felt it was his greatest responsibility to help his mother to trust Christ, and he would have been prepared to give anything for this. Now his joy was boundless.

As his mother slowly weakened physically, so she grew closer to him and Jennifer. Only near the end did they all realise how much they loved each other, so grieving happened almost more before her death than afterwards. The anguish was while she was in hospital, unable to communicate or even eat properly. Peter even prayed, 'Lord, take her out of this.' When she died it was like the com-

pletion of a chapter, and Peter and Jennifer did not feel
they owed it to his mother to grieve unduly, as if they had
to prove their love by so doing. Their feeling was one of
peace, and such gratitude that she did not linger too
long. The greatest agony would have been if his mother
had died without faith.

As Peter sat crying by his mother's side a few minutes
after her death, Jennifer found that lovely book *Living
Light* at the bedside. The reading for that day, a Sunday,
began with the words from Job 19:25, 'I know that my
Redeemer lives,' and went on with Paul's words in 1
Corinthians 15:19–20: 'If only for this life we have hope
in Christ, we are to be pitied more than all men. But
Christ has indeed been raised from the dead, the first-
fruits of those who have fallen asleep.' For weeks before
she had died, Peter's mother had been unable to speak at
all. A couple of days before her death, a friend had sat
with her and started to read Psalm 23. 'The Lord is my
shepherd,' he began. Before he could continue, this
dying, speechless lady said quietly and distinctly, 'I shall
not want.' What splendid words with which to make a last
farewell to life on earth!

There is a rightness in death, and Peter and Jennifer
discovered it that Sunday. Which brings me back to my own
gran. Americans, in their sports, have someone they choose
as the MVP – the Most Valuable Player. In our family,
Gran would have been our MVP. Part of her value was
her longevity. She was seriously old! She was our link with
history, and I know second hand from her of life in 1815,
because she told me of her great-grandfather telling her
about the national rejoicing at the victory at the Battle of
Waterloo. From her birth in 1887 to her death in 1989
she lived through the reigns of six British monarchs.

What a love she showed us all! Whenever we fell out,
she would be the reconciler. If anyone in the family

of a younger generation died, she would say, 'I wish I'd been the one.' And whenever any one of us ventured to dare to do something for God, no one would encourage us more than Gran. Her simple faith in him pervaded all she did. So when she came to face her own death, she was ready. She even said to us, 'I wish I could die.' At 101, she had simply worn out. My father delightfully likened her to a lawn-mower. When you mow with a petrol-driven lawn-mower, it does not stop immediately when the fuel gets low. It stops and starts, chugging and getting slower. Gran was like that: she got slower and slower and finally chugged to a halt.

So Gran was ready for death: it was the most natural thing in the world. In the end she was tired, and ready for 'home'. My dad, who was seventy-five by the time his mother died, said how sorry he was to lose her but, 'You can't hang on for ever. I was happy to let her go – she had fulfilled her life.' After such a good innings there was no need for many tears. After such a glorious life, the words of John Milton in *Samson Agonistes* came to mind. Samson's father, Manoa, had just been told of his son's death, and Milton had him say:

> Nothing is here for tears, nothing to wail
> Or knock the breast; no weakness, no contempt,
> Dispraise, or blame; nothing but well and fair,
> And what may quiet us in a death so noble.

In the end, death does seem right. It is, quite simply, a door to a greater life in the eternity of God's immediate presence. That lovely children's book, *Badger's Parting Gifts* (published by Harper Collins), reminds one so touchingly that a full life leaves behind so many good things and so many special reminders that bereavement can give way to the joy of wonderful memories, and the happiness left for those still alive.

We ought not to cling too long to the life that goes to its deserved rest. I love God's promise to Abraham: 'You, however, will go to your fathers in peace and be buried at a good old age' (Genesis 15:15). And as our elderly relative or friend goes to their peace, so we may hear again the words of Jesus, as he faced his death: 'Peace I leave with you; my peace I give you. I do not give to you as the world gives. Do not let your hearts be troubled and do not be afraid' (John 14:27). As the one who then died, and was raised to live for ever, his eternal peace is for us today.

3

'. . . He's My Brother'

Derby, in March. Not the place nor the time for earth-shattering events. But this city in the North Midlands of England was the place and March was the month for life-shattering news for me.

I had gone there to speak to several hundred young people at a huge Youth for Christ rally, and was getting ready for the meeting when the phone rang. It was my wife, and she sounded deeply concerned.

'It's Keith. There's been an accident. They're trying to reach you from Nairobi. They say he's dying.'

My brother had flown to East Africa to be a doctor in Uganda a fortnight earlier, so I immediately called his missionary society in London. Details were sketchy, but, 'Yes, it's true. Keep in touch, and we'll let you have news as it comes in. Keith is being kept alive by hand-pumping a life-support system. There's no power in the village where he is.'

That's how the crushing news was broken to me. I was numbed with shock. Like the Psalm-writer 3,000 years ago, I cried to the Lord in my trouble (Psalm 107:28). And so began days of chaos and nights of pain, alternating between frantic efforts at phoning and restless waiting.

But who was Keith? As far as I can remember, he was the first tiny baby I'd ever seen. I was only three-and-three-quarters when he was born, so a baby brother was someone very special. When he was about three or so, we found he had a speech impediment. At least, the others said he had, though I could understand him perfectly – so I translated for him. That's probably why he never stopped talking when the impediment was put right!

When he was about eight, he got the chicken-pox. I heard him tell the story himself many times. When he was recovering he read a book about a boy to whom God gave a new heart. The boy in the story told his sister, who said to him, 'Show it to me.' Keith said that on reading the story, he also wanted a new heart – so he asked God for one. And that's when he became a Christian.

It didn't stop him being a scatterbrain. He managed to ride my bike in front of a car when he was eleven, and get a triple fracture of the femur. But he survived – albeit with his right leg over an inch shorter than the left.

And from the age of eight he always wanted to be a missionary doctor. He wasn't one of those geniuses at school, but eventually, after a lot of hard work and sweat, he got to St Thomas's Hospital in London, where he trained and eventually qualified as a doctor. While he was there, he had to do ten weeks at another hospital. Instead of a lucrative trip to the States, he chose to go to a village hospital at Amudat in Uganda. When he qualified he went there again for three months before his first houseman's job.

Then, after working for a while in hospitals in this country, he received a letter one day. It was from Amudat. 'President Amin has expelled the only qualified white member of our hospital,' it said. 'Please come and be our doctor.' I'd known Keith long enough to realise that his being a Christian was no mere theory – he'd follow Jesus Christ wherever he called and whatever it cost. After obtaining the necessary work permit, he flew to

Kampala and motored to his new life as a doctor to 40,000 people in north-east Uganda.

After a fortnight, he found that the medical supplies were desperately inadequate, so he motored 300 miles back to Kampala in a hospital truck to stock up. He returned through the night and slept by the roadside, then at 5am he continued his journey. Unknown to Keith, an Italian doctor had overturned his own truck two hours before on a notorious bend at a place with the splendid name of Nakapiripiriti. Keith rounded the bend in his vehicle and, in avoiding the overturned truck, turned over himself. He said to his passenger – who was uninjured – 'Let's pray,' and they did. Then he sent the man for help, and fell unconscious. When help arrived he was carted dozens of miles through the bush to a missionary outpost, where they worked his chest by hand to get him to breathe. He had broken the base of his skull. That was the news I gradually received from almost impossible phone links with the border region of Kenya and Uganda. They were doing all they could, they said, and I knew they were.

What could I do? I was so helpless. It sounds trite to say that I could pray, but I did a lot of that. 'Oh God, be with Keith. Lord, if you take him – he's yours. And if you give him back – he's yours. I don't own him.' But there was another prayer, too, which I know others in the family prayed. 'Lord, don't let Keith be a "cabbage". Please let him be really well – or take him home to yourself.' It would have been too dreadful for him to be a pale shadow of his vibrant self. We asked friends to pray that, too.

Of course, life has to go on, even when the news is so desperate. Impending death makes everything chaotic. It is mind-numbing. It changes plans and lives, sometimes for ever. But the Youth for Christ rally in Derby still needed a speaker, and that speaker was still me. I arrived late. I'm told they were extremely surprised I arrived at all. I told them my brother's story, and people still come up to me today and remind me of that evening, when they were challenged as to their own relationship with God, and whether they were prepared to die.

Back in Manchester where we lived, work went on, too. I was grateful for an understanding boss, who gave me some time off to carry on with my phoning. A huge complication lay in the fact that my father was on the other side of the world. As Town Clerk of Harrogate, Yorkshire, he was on his way to their 'twin' city of Wellington, New Zealand. I caught him at his hotel in Sydney, Australia, en route.

How could I tell my dear dad that his son was dying? Only ten years earlier we'd lost Mum – and now this. Poor Dad.

'What shall I do?' he asked.

'You'd never forgive yourself if you didn't try to get to him,' I replied. 'So go to Africa. I'll call you half way in New Delhi.' Somehow Dad got through on the phone to Dr Peter Cox in Kapenguria.

Peter and his team were keeping Keith alive artificially by hand; a task they continued in relays for about thirty-six hours. Peter told Dad that there was little point in their going on, and that he would shortly have to pronounce Keith dead. My dad is rarely an outwardly emotional man. But when he put the phone down he did what he has only ever done once again (when he touched the rock in the Garden of Gethsemane in Jerusalem where Jesus knelt to pray before the crucifixion). Dad broke into uncontrollable sobbing in his hotel room at 2am. It was probably the best thing he could have done, for he says that after that he had no sense of deep grief.

We made contact at New Delhi, where we cried

together on the phone as I broke the news that Keith had indeed died. In some ways it was a relief that Keith had been released.

There can be no doubt that to lose a child is a catastrophic thing. Dad says you actually lose part of yourself, and you can never fully understand it until it happens to you. Part of you dies, physically and emotionally.

On the onward flight to Nairobi, Dad composed himself enough to enable him to fly in the Missionary Aviation Fellowship plane up to Kitale for the funeral. Bishop Brian Herd, Bishop of Karamoja, came over to Kenya to take the funeral. He had only recently been appointed Bishop, and it was no easy task. Working under the regime of Idi Amin ultimately led to the bishop and his wife escaping from Uganda under serious death threats. Even today Bishop Herd and his wife Norma speak of the 'tremendous sense of loss in Uganda' when Keith died, and what a sobering time it was. At least five other church workers there had died in the years immediately preceding Keith's death.

It is at times like these that Christianity proves itself. The bishop recalls how the local Christians and the missionaries saw all these deaths as being a beginning, not an end. How impressed he was when Dad actually spoke at Keith's funeral. Keith's body was laid to rest in a quiet corner of the missionary graveyard, alongside the grave of Dr Graham Fraser, a previous doctor at Amudat, who had died in not dissimilar circumstances. The leaders of the church at Amudat had walked forty or fifty miles to Kitale to be at the funeral. 'Would it be possible,' they asked the bishop, 'for Dr Keith's father to come up to Amudat?'

'No, that is out of the question,' said Bishop Herd. 'Mr Knox has travelled too far already.'

However, Dad had other ideas – so off they went.

Daudi, the African pastor, was overjoyed. 'The bishop say "no". God say "yes". Dr Keith's father is here!' he told the crowded church where Keith was so loved. Even the Amin hierarchy wrote of Keith: 'He was a young intelligent man, full of vigour and determination to treat the sick as well as to spread the word of God in South Karamoja. His death has caused a great loss to us all in the Ministry of Health.'

Meanwhile, back in England, the rest of the family was struggling to come to terms with the enormity of events on another continent, as were friends and acquaintances. My other brother, Martin, who was twenty at the time, was studying law at Sheffield University. He first heard the news of Keith when the warden of his hall of residence told him, 'Your brother's had a really serious accident. He's broken his neck and is in a coma.' So he did what he thought a good Christian should do – be a good witness to his Christian faith by chatting normally and acting as if nothing had happened! But part of him couldn't believe what was happening, and he had a sinking feeling of unreality, as if his personality had split in half – the outward 'show' and the inward unbelief.

Happily, he found a solution. He phoned a Christian couple, who invited him over. They let him talk and talk about Keith, and asked him to stay the night. Martin said he felt cared for and can still 'feel' the pyjamas Bob lent him! Of course he wept, but got through because others cared so much. 'I was buoyed up on a sea of the prayers of God's people,' is how he describes it. His memories now are not of sorrow, nor of Keith's death, but of the good times.

My sister, Sue, had a similar experience. She was working as a nurse in a doctors' practice. The senior partner asked her to come round and bring her photo album. He talked with her about the happy times – with Keith and with her husband: 'Go home and tell your old man he's beautiful – think of the living and not the dead.'

The impact of Keith's death outside the immediate family was enormous. No less than six memorial services were held – two in hospitals where he had worked. The family put no obituary in the paper, but one appeared in the *Yorkshire Evening Post*. Keith had been a houseman at the famous St James' Hospital, Leeds ('Jimmy's'), where he had perpetually been dragged out of bed by his 'bleep' going off, calling him to yet another emergency. The obituary read: 'Dr Keith Knox. With our love to his family. The happiest voice on bleep. St James' telephonists.'

Among the young people in Knaresborough, Yorkshire, where Keith had been the youth leader, were several who gave their lives to the Lord Jesus as a result of Keith's death. They believed that if Keith could die in the service of Jesus Christ, they could live for that same Jesus. For others, it stirred memories of similar situations through which they themselves had passed. American evangelist Billy Graham's right-hand man in Britain, Maurice Rowlandson, had lost a daughter in a car accident, and wrote as a family friend to assure us that God is faithful and able to help us, as he had helped them. Maurice's encouragement and caution was, 'The wound will heal, but the scar will always be there.'

How did Keith himself face death? Did he know he would die? Obviously in going to Uganda he must have foreseen the possibility. Before he left England, he invited fifty friends to a party, which turned out to be quite an event. Not to put too fine a point on it, he acted the complete idiot. He organised all the games, including one where everyone had to shout as loudly as they could, and he would out-shout the whole room. With his voice, he almost certainly won.

Having got everyone completely worked up, he asked for silence. Very quietly, he told how he had gone into Knaresborough Parish Church the previous day to pray. There he had seen a memorial to one of the martyrs of the Reformation. On his way to being burned to death at the stake, this Christian martyr had turned to his daughter and said, 'Pray for me, as I will pray for thee, that we might meet merrily in heaven.' So Keith took his own farewell – and went straight back to the rumbustiousness of the party. Yet it was those quiet words that people remember most: Dad still quotes them at family prayers each day.

Why did he die? The obvious answer is because his truck overturned. Death is a normal part of life. But as to the deeper, underlying question, I have never seen it better answered than in an article written shortly after Keith's death by The Revd David Kirkwood. He was editor of *Mission*, the house magazine of Keith's society, The Bible Churchman's Missionary Society (BCMS). He wrote:

> The shock of his death and the deep sadness at so untimely a loss when he was needed so much in Uganda, prompt the same questions as some of the disciples asked when the box of ointment was broken over the head of Jesus. 'To what purpose is this waste?' (Mark 14:4). But such questioning was silenced by the Lord. 'And the house was filled with the fragrance.' In the tender, understanding presence of the Lord, our griefs and disappointments are soothed by a deep sense of his constant love and the wisdom of all that he allows. And the fragrance of Keith's robust, dedicated life will long linger on to remind us of a very dear young friend.

Dad has a similar approach. When he himself was young, he heard the story of a gardener who had a garden he tended at some great house. In this garden he had one most beautiful rose, which was his pride and joy. One day the rose was gone, and he was distraught. 'Who took my rose?' he asked. 'The master,' was the reply. The story concluded, 'And the gardener held his peace.' So Dad has no anger, no bitterness. But often he will see a bearded young man in the street and for a split second think – 'Keith!'

For myself, I think of the good times we had and the inspiration Keith still is to me. Whenever I feel like quitting, I see Keith in the front row of our church trying to out-sing the whole choir – and succeeding. I hear him shouting out the good news of Jesus on the beach at Whitby. And I draw strength from the God who was *his* God. And I regain my perspective. Occasionally, I find myself trying to out-sing a church choir during 'Love divine, all loves excelling', or 'Hark the herald angels sing', and my voice seems to choke as my thoughts are with Keith.

A couple of months after his death, I was asked to speak on television about him. I concluded what I said with these words:

> When he was young he had a lovely treble voice, and our Great Aunt Ada made him sing for her. Their joint favourite was 'The Old Rugged Cross':
>
> > So I'll cherish the old rugged cross,
> > And exchange it one day for a crown.
>
> He had cherished the cross of Christ – as a boy and as a man. In the end it was the only thing that mattered – and in the end it's the only thing that will matter for any of us.
>
> > That's why, on 6th March 1976, Dr Keith Knox won a crown of glory. He was my brother.

4

A Child Dies

One of the bravest things ever said was by a man called Job. He had just received the most terrible news: his children had been killed when the house they were in collapsed in a storm. In great grief he fell on the ground, and yet was able to say, 'The Lord gave and the Lord has taken away; may the name of the Lord be praised' (Job 1:21).

I have often wondered at his courage, and his reaction to such a tragedy. What would anyone say if that were to happen to them today? So far in this book we have looked at deaths which, though very sad, are nevertheless to be expected. Sooner or later our grandparents and parents will die, and so will our partners – unless we die first. There is a natural sequence of dying. But how do you manage when a death happens which is apparently out of the right order of things, especially when the life taken from you is of someone much younger in years? This was brought home to me recently when a close friend of our twelve-year-old son, Andrew, was killed on his way home from school.

Ian and Andrew had a great last year at junior school. Together with another friend, Callum, and Ian's dad, they had spent many evenings after school building an electric car. Not quite finished when summer came, the

46

four decided they would get together in the autumn to complete the project, even though they would then be in different senior schools. So in the September of 1991, Ian went off to his new school, glad to be a 'senior' at last, and he settled well into his new environment. Then on 19th September, on his way home from school, he was crossing a busy dual carriageway when he was hit by a car. When I talked with Mike, Ian's father, it was just over one year since the accident.

On that Thursday afternoon, Mike was picking up his younger son, Stephen, from the nearby junior school. Someone told him of Ian's accident, and he rushed over, to find the ambulance leaving. Mike followed to the hospital, where his wife Sue joined him. Waiting to hear news always seems to go on for hours, and Ian had to be transferred to another hospital for a brain scan, which meant more delay. Eventually he was put on a life-support machine, and was monitored every twenty minutes as hospital staff fought for his survival. He never recovered consciousness, and died three days later. Throughout those three days of hope and despair, tears flowed freely. In the shock of what had happened, Mike did not eat throughout, and yet felt no hunger. None of the family slept.

Sue was in deep shock, and could not accept that Ian would not come back, though the doctor tried to help her face reality with the brutal truth. Somehow Mike realised Ian would not survive. How could any good come out of what was happening? Then the thought occurred to him: what about allowing some of Ian's internal organs to be used to save someone else's life? To his considerable surprise, Stephen told Mike how Ian carried his own donor card, and how he himself had wanted to help another in exactly this way. Stephen, though only eight, was insistent, and so Ian's liver and kidneys were given after his death to help other people live.

In the meantime, the fight for Ian went on, but by the Sunday he was deteriorating fast. Sue went in to see her son alone, and felt more calm afterwards. By this time Ian was diagnosed brain-dead, and the only decision left was when to disconnect the life-support machine. Finally there was no alternative and, with a deep grief, they learned of Ian's death at 1am. He was eleven years old. As the family left the hospital, Sue passed out. 'She's switched off,' explained the hospital chaplain, and they took her back inside to sleep. Mike went to look at Ian, who seemed so much at rest and in peace, with the noisy machine silent at last.

Mike remembers little of the funeral, except for row upon row of flowers; he was still giddy with shock. My wife, who went to the funeral with our Andrew, said that all went well till the final hymn, the lovely children's song 'Lord of the Dance', when most of the congregation burst into tears.

So how have Sue and Mike survived this tragedy of an untimely death, and of losing a son just as his life was opening out before him? They have shed many tears, which is a relief. It has helped them to talk about it with friends, and together. Indeed, it is at times like this that 'you realise who your real friends are', says Mike. Even talking with the driver of the car which was involved in the accident and consoling her was positive. They let her know they felt no bitterness towards her, and that they agreed with the coroner's verdict of 'Accidental Death'.

Anger is vented on silly things, like not being able to find a pen, but work has proved a therapeutic occupation for Mike, as has trying to get back to normal life as soon as possible. There are too many happy memories of Ian for bitterness, and even the three days of Ian's dying brought Mike closer to him. Mike still feels a bond, and he thinks that this may be because of God's help. However, Mike did not consciously turn to God for help, then or afterwards, though he cannot speak too highly of the help given by the hospital chaplain. Even in his worst moments Mike did not cry to God. 'My tears are for Ian,' he says. Today, Mike says he will always be scarred, but it is getting easier.

And what of our son Andrew's feelings? Ian had been a good friend – they had been two of the Three Kings in the Christmas pageant at school! Now they were looking forward to finishing their great car, which had already won competitions for its design and which, when they were twelve, they would be able to race. On that fateful Thursday Andrew went down to another friend's house to be greeted with the dreadful news of the accident. For Andrew this was a first. It was his first funeral, and he found it 'weird'. He was interested to see how people reacted, and that people who hardly knew Ian had cried. Andrew's main problem has been realising how death changes things for ever. It is hard for him to imagine not having his cheerful, joking friend around. Of course, he never imagined Ian would die, and shuddered when he had to believe it.

And Andrew is sorry. He is sorry especially, he says, for Ian's mum, particularly as she has the added burden of being deaf, and for the problems and hurts felt by the family. He is sorry to have lost the friendship he had. And he is sorry they will never finish their great car because, as Mike says, there is too much of Ian in it for them to go on. But, as Andrew philosophically told me, everyone has to die, and there is nothing you can do about it. If good can come from such a tragedy, one of the good things I have seen has been the mature and Christian way in which our son has faced Ian's death, as it will strengthen him for future bereavements.

Personally I find great strength in the splendid incident in Matthew 18, where the disciples are arguing over who is the greatest in the kingdom of heaven. Jesus, we read, called a little child, had him stand among them, and said, 'I tell you the truth, unless you change and become like little children, you will never enter the kingdom of heaven' (Matthew 18:3). On another occasion, Jesus put this even more strongly: 'Let the little children come to me, and do not hinder them, for the kingdom of God belongs to such as these' (Mark 10:14). Ian, as a child, is assured of his home in heaven. We need to have a childlike faith in Jesus, to be sure we will be there too.

If this recent death of Ian has been hard to live with, then Corrine's story is, if possible, even worse. In 1985, Vilma and Anthony were living in Coventry with their children Craig, then thirteen, and Corrine aged ten. They were a closely-knit, happy Christian family. One day during half-term, Vilma took Craig shopping, while Anthony stayed at home to fix the car. The car was up on ramps, when somehow it jumped the ramps, just as Corrine came round the corner on roller skates. Anthony watched in helpless horror as Corrine fell, hitting her head on the kerb. She died instantaneously. An ambulance was called, and she was whisked away, while Anthony waited for his church minister to take him to the hospital. While waiting, he went to the bathroom to get cleaned up from his car repairing. His simple prayer was, 'Lord Jesus, be with her.' 'And he was,' says Anthony.

He prayed with the minister before they left, but wishes now that they had prayed for a miracle. Today, Vilma cannot read about the incident in the Bible where Jesus brought back to life a twelve-year-old girl. At the hospital, Corrine had already been certified dead, and a policeman broke the news to Anthony in tears. Meanwhile,

Vilma had arrived back from shopping to find the street full of people, and neighbours trying to take her into their houses. The minister's wife drove her to hospital, where a silent shake of Anthony's head confirmed her worst fears. 'I knew it would happen,' Vilma said. 'All my life I somehow knew something would happen, and I knew from that moment that life would never be the same again.'

Anthony's immediate reaction was to blame himself, but Vilma told him at once that she never wanted to hear that again – it was no one's fault. Corrine's death hit Vilma like a physical blow when a nurse asked, 'What was her name?' It was the tense of the verb, and Vilma replied, 'Her name is Corrine.' Vilma wishes she could have sat with Corrine, even for a few minutes, but she had no strength to ask to stay. 'I regret I couldn't stay longer, but it was total shock, shock, shock.'

That October Tuesday was followed so quickly by a Friday funeral. It was rushed, but they felt it was better than dragging it out. The formalities were methodical, but there is no preparation for this sort of event, and if some warning had been given, things might have been done differently. Was cremation right? If only there were a grave to go to now. They asked everyone at the funeral to wear light, bright colours – pink if possible. At the door of the church, the steward gave Anthony a single pink rose, which he placed on the coffin during the service. Today, on the anniversary of Corrine's death, and on her birthday, Vilma buys ten pink roses for their home, and puts them by Corrine's photo. Vilma has been singing Christian music for a number of years, both as a soloist and leader of a choir, and she has now recorded a tape of her own called 'Roses in Heaven'.

At the time, the family was swept along on a tide, as others did the thinking for them. They proved the huge value of being part of a Christian community, of living in a village where they were known, and of having had a much-loved daughter. As Mary in Chapter 1 discovered, the people most able to help were those who had suffered a similar tragedy: a couple whose son had died, aged seven. Numb with shock, they nevertheless had a sense of God sweeping them along, with everyone saying how wonderfully they were being upheld by God. 'But,' they honestly told me, 'it was like hell. And if God had *not* been holding us up it would have been *real* hell.'

In other words, it was easier because God was around, but it was still awful, and is so today. Their experience is that God does not make everything OK just like that, but that God was in it with them, and that made the difference. They were most comforted in finding a hidden message from Corrine. She had found a slit in the wallpaper above her bed, and slipped into it a tiny piece of folded paper on which she had written, 'Jesus is my best friend. I know that he loves me. He helps me when I'm feeling sad. I know he loves me.' The *Coventry Evening Telegraph*, reporting Corrine's accident, printed her note in full. Lots of messages from friends helped too, and they surrounded the family like a blanket. 'But the pain burns you up as the blanket goes cold,' says Vilma.

Anthony still asks God why Corrine had to die. 'It's the fist-waving syndrome,' he admits. He believed Corrine was a gift from God, and saw her as being on loan, but does not like the fact that the loan was then called in. Why would God need her? Weren't her family's needs greater? Vilma has changed her mind. At first she thought that God had taken Corrine. Now she sees that we live in a sin-sick world, and death is part of it. Life in such a world is tenuous, transient and imperfect, and these things happen. I believe Vilma is right.

If we can do something positive as the result of a person's death, it can help considerably. So it was for Vilma and Anthony when they established a fund in Corrine's memory, the proceeds going to the Anglican Hospice for Children at Helen House, Oxford. As someone caring for dying children, the head of the hospice wrote to the family, 'You never get over the death of a child, but in time, a long, long time, you learn to adjust.'

This has proved true. They have never 'got over' Corrine's death, though they sensed other people wanted them to. They thought time would heal, but they sank into an abyss. Slowly they realised they did not have to get over it, rather they had to adjust, and live their lives without Corrine. There are still times when they grieve and hurt, but they have learned to cope with pain. The pain never goes away completely, but they have gained a quality of life which is worthwhile, and they know God's love. They thank God for the ten years they shared with Corrine, and for such happiness and blessings. They thank God for each other, and for friends who care. But oh how they wish for a rebellious teenage daughter. . . .

So they find it is a good idea to avoid too much contact with the past – the tapes of Corrine singing, or a video of her. And yet Anthony finds joy in coming down to the kitchen each morning, looking at her photo and quietly greeting her with a 'Hi Corrine!'. And when he told me, even Vilma did not know he did that! Vilma and Anthony think a lot about heaven and seeing Corrine again. We either let the pain make us bitter, or we let God use it. They have chosen the latter. They are brave people. 'Who shall separate us from the love of Christ?' asks the Bible.

Shall trouble or hardship or persecution? . . . No, in all these things we are more than conquerors through him

who loved us. For I am convinced that neither death nor life
. . . nor any powers . . . nor anything else in all creation, will
be able to separate us from the love of God that is in Christ
Jesus our Lord (Romans 8:35, 37–39).

Now let me tell you why I had a personal interest in this
chapter. Because this experience almost happened to us.

Land-speed records are there to be broken, and I may
be the holder of the fastest drive up the M1 motorway in
England in a Renault 5. If I had been stopped by a policeman, I would have asked him to help me go even faster!
And why this motorway madness? I was responding to a
desperate phone-call from my wife, who told me our son
Jon, then just three, was being rushed into hospital. Jon
had got the measles, and was not getting better, refusing
to eat or drink, and just lying in bed. My wife, Ruth, had
insisted that the doctor come round, despite it being the
Easter Bank Holiday weekend. Grudgingly he agreed – it
was not usual to look at a measles case. Within two
minutes of his arriving, however, the doctor cleared the
stairs in two leaps to call for an ambulance, for here was a
child with chronic pneumonia and possible meningitis.

In the ambulance Ruth cradled Jon on her lap, leaving
his older brother Matthew with her mother, who was staying with us. Jon was rushed to an isolation ward where,
because of his dehydration, he was put on a drip, and
given injections because he could not keep down any
medicine. Soon afterwards, I arrived from a curtailed
conference after my spectacular drive, to find our son
thin, pale and very ill. He lay there looking pathetic. His
weight had fallen from over forty pounds to twenty-one –
less than he had weighed at eighteen months.

To stare death in the face is a terrible thing. At the conference I had bought a poster, intended for Jon's bedroom, showing a baby duckling in a jacket breast pocket,

with the message, 'Lord, protect me, and keep me close
to your heart.' It seemed so appropriate to put it up next
to his bed, as I took the other bed in the isolation ward to
be with him through each night. Poor Ruth felt as any
mother would – if only it could have been her going
through it instead of him. She hoped and prayed she had
got him there in time. He was too ill to complain of the
huge injections he was being given.

The crisis came to a head at midnight on Easter Saturday. The nurse was due to give him another injection,
and I somehow knew that this was it. Jon was slowly slip-
ping away, and there was little I could do. As the nurse
got to the foot of the bed, I held his tiny, helpless hands,
and said the only thing I could: 'Lord, if you take him,
he's yours. And if you give him back, he's yours.' Perhaps
God had been waiting for me to get to that point, because
at that moment I felt as if Jon and I were held tightly
within the arms of a loving Father, and all was well, whatever happened. Miracles do happen, and Jon came back.
However, as we saw in Chapter 3 concerning my brother,
an identical prayer can lead to the other result, too.

But Jon's skirmish with death did teach me that no one
'belongs' to me. As Anthony and Vilma felt, our children
are on loan, and each person is ultimately God's concern. Their destiny is up to them, and him. What I had to
do, and still need to, is entrust my family to God, and not
worry over-much for them, though Chapter 9 will show
how I have, more recently, had to face this one again.
However, this does not remove our parental responsibility: Ruth and I have, of course, cared for Jon, and our
other children, before and since then. We nursed him
through his recovery, and we have brought him up, seeking to lead him in God's way, and helping him to grow to
be a man. We firmly believe in God's instruction, 'Train a
child in the way he should go, and when he is old he will

not turn from it' (Proverbs 22:6). But Jon is God's – we gave him to God. When I see him now in the middle of a rugby scrum, that fact is a cause for considerable relief!

5

Only a Baby

If anyone had asked me, before I started researching this book, which kind of bereavement would have produced most visible grief as people told me their stories, I would never have guessed right. I might have made a suggestion that it would be suicide, or divorce, or the death of a child. In fact the loss of a baby proved to be a long way ahead of the rest. Never say to anyone whose baby has just died, or who has had a miscarriage, 'Oh well, it was only a baby!' because you may live to regret it. The person who has suffered such a loss will certainly regret it, very much.

Consider first the loss of a first child. After four years of marriage, Judy and Tony were thrilled to be expecting a baby. On a Sunday evening in March, the only problem seemed to be that the birth was by breech delivery. 'His heart is very strong,' Judy was told as Mark was born. Then the nursing staff rushed Tony out, a paediatrician ran in, Judy was given an injection and Mark was put in an incubator.

'It's all right,' they told Judy, as she went into unconsciousness. But she knew it was not so. Mark was, in fact, impossibly ill. No one knew if he had had enough oxygen, and various organs in his body had not formed in the womb. Someone finally told Tony, out in the corridor, that his baby was very ill. But when he started to cry, the only comment was, 'Pull yourself together. There are other patients here.' What was he supposed to do? After phoning his church for prayer, he asked to see the baby, and found three or four nurses round the incubator. There was his beautiful son, looking perfect: all the problems were on the inside.

It seems almost crazy, but Judy was never shown her son. Eighteen years later she is still angry. Not only that, no one told her Mark had died, until Tony went back to her, dissolved into tears and asked her, 'What are we going to do?' He assumed she knew. They held on to each other, and a Christian friend arrived and prayed with them. Finally a doctor stood in the doorway. 'I'm sorry to have to tell you your little boy has died.' It was the first verbal communication to Judy that anything was wrong.

After the initial shock, Judy did not fall apart. Like my brother when our mum died, Judy felt buoyed up on the prayers of her church and friends. As so often happens, some people did not know what to say, and so avoided them. Tony would go over to neighbours and tell them, 'It's OK to talk to us!' One of his hardest moments was the one which all who lose a baby at birth share in common: registering the birth and the death at the same time. The Registrar did not say a word. Compared with that, the hospital staff did behave better in the end, and were concerned for the well-being not just of Judy, their patient, but of Tony too. The church was fantastic, though Judy struggled with all the flowers, wanting them to die so she could get on with life.

The funeral was a relief, enabling there to be a letting go. The period of shock was like a dream world, and when Judy woke during the night her arms would ache physically, and she would cry. Years later she would find herself in tears as she suddenly remembered Mark. And

even now, with three lovely daughters, Tony will sometimes say he has four children. How have they got over it?
Judy accepted Mark's death as a fact, and she now suffers
no emotional traumas. She had to overcome her feeling
of failure for never giving Tony a son, even to the extent
of praying that at least one of the girls would be a boy.
She has latterly been helped, surprisingly, by her father's
death. He became a Christian as a result of Mark's death,
and Judy pictures her two special men being together in
heaven.

Tony still grieves, and wept as we spoke together all
these years later. He has wanted a son so much, though
would not swap one of his daughters. The birth of their
first daughter did help greatly, and Judy was glad Debbie
was not a boy, so that she could not be considered a substitute for Mark. Tony is now a vicar, and his awful experience enables him to sympathise with all who grieve,
especially in helping the families of children who die. But
he is hurt when he looks back. Perhaps the difference
between them is that Judy looks back and remembers
tears and pain, but Tony relives it, because he has no son.

Judy and Tony draw consolation and sure hope from
the verse I quoted in the last chapter: 'Unless you change
and become like little children, you will never enter the
kingdom of heaven' (Matthew 18:3). Our babies do go to
heaven – but it is hard not to see them grow up here.

Would it have been easier, I wondered, if Tony and
Judy had later had a boy? I went to see John and Jo about
their daughter Heidi. Like Mark, Heidi was a first baby.
She died through an argument about dates. Jo and her
own doctor said the baby was due in September, but the
consultant favoured October and the consultant won.
Alas, by 21st October Jo was at forty-six weeks, according
to her own dates. In terrible pain one day, Jo realised
something dreadful had happened, and was rushed to

the maternity hospital. All her first-baby excitement had gone and terror reigned. The staff could find no heartbeat, and the doctor tried to tell Jo her baby was dead, as she screamed, 'Don't tell me!'

One can only guess at Jo's feelings as she had to go through labour, knowing no life would result. 'It was a total nightmare – nothing but shock and devastation,' Jo told me. Poor John was advised not to go in, so Jo was surrounded by strangers. Eleven years later she is still trying to come to terms with what happened, and her anger with the hospital, its staff and everyone involved. She was allowed to see her baby, who was very post-mature, and was able to hold her. But there was no funeral, and the hospital only spoke about a 'disposal'. Not being Christians, John and Jo saw no church minister, and had no counselling. Jo was taken back to the maternity ward, where she had to endure the heart-breaking sounds of living babies crying, till John discharged her and brought her home. Even seeing other babies afterwards was too much to cope with.

I asked Jo how she had survived. Two things helped. The first was having another daughter, born just before the first anniversary of Heidi's death. She was the first of three living children, and such a delight. And secondly, a couple of years ago, Jo and John became Christians, which has helped them to see that there is purpose in life, even in Heidi's death – though they are still waiting to find out what that purpose is. They are able to believe now that they will meet Heidi, alive and well, when they are united in God's eternal kingdom. They can also see that God's attitude to a baby dying is very different from the 'disposal' approach of the hospital. Our value before God is that stated by Jesus: 'Are not two sparrows sold for a penny? Yet not one of them will fall to the ground apart from the will of your Father. And even the very hairs of your head are all numbered. So don't be afraid; you are worth more than many sparrows' (Matthew 10:29–31). Heidi may only have seemed like a 'little sparrow', but she was, and is, precious to God.

Perhaps the problem for both these couples was that they had had no child previously. Would it not have eased the burden if they had already got a couple of children, and then a baby had died? Again, the answer is a resounding *no*.

Barry and Marion already had a ten-year-old son and a daughter of eight when, to their considerable surprise, Matthew was expected. For them, it was almost a bereavement to be *having* another baby, coming to terms with a major change in an established family's life. Then came excitement, and the plans and hopes of brother and sister. At twenty-two weeks, Marion got backache and an infection, which slowly became worse. Taken in to hospital, her waters broke. Despite all efforts, Matthew was born just before twenty-four weeks.

For Marion the birth was the worst point of all. Her body wanted to push, but her mind wanted to keep the baby till he was fully ready. Through her screams she told Barry how sorry she was, as if she were to blame. Barry and Marion had only been Christians a few years, and they so wanted to bring up a child in a Christian home from birth. In reading the Bible that morning, Barry had used some notes to explain what he had studied, and these had concluded with the words, 'The Lord will prepare you for any eventuality.' It was just as well, for Matthew, whose name means 'a gift from God', survived only nine hours.

I went to his funeral which was, as is always the case for a baby, a deeply emotional service, with the tiny white coffin a poignant symbol of the fragility of human life. The church surrounded the family with their love.

By comparison, the world out there was a hard place. The hospital lost Marion's records. An unfortunate midwife arrived at the home, asking, 'Right, where's the baby?' 'He died in hospital,' replied an appalled Barry. Each member of the family grieved differently, and it is important for bereaved families to realise that one person will react in a different way from another. One style of grief may suit one person, but we cannot expect a mirroring in our partner, or our child. Marion talked incessantly to anyone who would listen, and had to make the first move with other friends who were expecting babies, who did not know what to say to her. She had to recover from the guilt of having prayed, at the beginning, 'O God, don't let me be pregnant' – as if Matthew had died in answer to that prayer. Having had other bereavements, Marion understood there would be a pattern to her grieving, and went through what she called 'a normal two-year grief cycle'.

Poor Barry had a much worse time of it. Only his grandfather had died in his family, so this was his first real bereavement. Having to register the birth and the death at the same time, the lady in the Registry Office insensitively asked, 'I don't suppose you want the Birth Certificate?' 'To say I had a heavy heart is an understatement,' Barry says. He felt his position as a father, needing to protect his wife and children, which inhibited personal grief. But he and Marion did feel carried along by God, as if on a cloud. People would come to the house in tears, and leave smiling. They felt able to praise God for Matthew's brief life.

It did not last. Barry grew increasingly bitter, and a dreadful year followed. The rest of the family seemed to recover, and so needed his support less. And Barry felt, wrongly as it transpired, that his church and friends were not supporting him. In grief, it is hard to see what we, or others, are doing. When visitors called, Barry would disappear down to the greenhouse, not wanting to talk. Some friends would call too often, and others, seeing visitors present, did not want to over-crowd. Barry's shutters came up, even to Marion.

Barry dropped out of the church, angry with people who were, in fact, caring and praying. In the end he received a ticking-off from God! 'You are in a cesspit of self-pity, looking to others and not to me,' he heard God say. He phoned his vicar, saying that he wanted to rededicate his life to the Lord. He and his family have been wonderfully restored, and can now praise God again. 'I carry a scar, but the scab has dropped off,' is how Barry describes it. And he has found the love he thought he had lost, and the friends who had always wanted to love him, but had been repelled.

And the children? With no sense of bitterness, their son told me he is still upset, and his feelings have changed little since Matthew's death. For the daughter, a big, crazy dog called Hamish has joined the family, and given her someone else to befriend and love. The whole family knows all is well for Matthew, recalling the lovely words when Jesus 'took the children in his arms, put his hands on them and blessed them' (Mark 10:16). Luke makes it clear that this included 'babies' (Luke 18:15).

If Barry took a year out to grieve, that was nothing compared to Ann when her son Michael died at six months. Married two years to Roger, all seemed well till Michael was four weeks old, when a fortnight of investigations led to his admission to hospital with a serious heart deformity. For over four months Ann visited Michael three times a day. When he died, even the staff nurse wept as she handed over the papers. As we have seen before, those who have similarly suffered are the best help, and

non-church neighbours who had lost a child gave support, while some Christians felt they had to be 'spiritual'
rather than practical, and tended to back away. Good
counsel was given that Ann and Roger should not adopt
in an attempt to replace Michael, but Ann can now
understand the pressure which causes some women to
steal babies.

We will meet Ann and Roger again in Chapter 15,
when their life with their next child is described, with her
severe handicap. This extra burden, under two years
later, certainly contributed to the huge length of time
Ann took to recover from Michael's death. With work to
return to, the fear of having another baby, the pain of a
perfect second child receiving an injection which went
wrong at eleven months – all these help to explain Ann's
struggle. 'You can't grieve to order,' says Ann.

Her big mistake was to exclude God, by a deliberate act
of will, when Michael went into hospital. Although a keen
Christian, Ann turned her back on God, put her Bible
away, and saw no point in praying with Roger. Roger shed
many tears, but got on with life and stuck in with the
church. Ann kept away from church, and got to the point
where there was nothing left to life, except bitterness
inside. She became afraid of everything, and angry to
think that other people could live a worthwhile life while
she could not. Maybe counselling would have helped.
Ann looks back on 'fourteen wasted years', and is
relieved to be back. (You will have to wait till Chapter 15
to read how she made it!) Suffice to say, we need to fall
apart as quickly as we can, accept help offered, and not
block out the God who loves us. Especially because, if our
baby has died, death may have been better for that child,
even though the loss is dreadful for us. There is comfort
in these lovely words about God: 'He tends his flock like a
shepherd: He gathers the lambs in his arms and carries

them close to his heart; he gently leads those that have young' (Isaiah 40:11). After what seemed like for ever, Ann would now agree!

When it comes to the loss of a baby, there is another kind of death which is just as hurtful – death before birth. 'Paul' and 'Linda' married when they were a little bit older, so they were keen to have children sooner rather than later. Within a month, Linda was pregnant, but the pregnancy only lasted twelve weeks. They felt awful. Linda had lost something that was part of her; someone with whom they were looking forward to making a family. Compared with a baby arriving, even one who died almost at once, there was the added shock and numbness of coming to terms with losing someone they had never seen. There was no funeral service, and nothing tangible to show for their grieving. Linda looked the same when she left hospital as when she went in, but she had lost something precious.

Depression set in and lasted some months, but Paul and Linda could not talk about a person. There were no photos, and life for everyone else seemed to go on as normal. A second miscarriage followed two years later, and then came a final try, which they knew was their last chance. Linda saw the doctor, had hormone treatment and lay in bed. Then a scan showed that something was terribly wrong, and that she would miscarry again. This duly happened. 'It's not fair. Everyone else can and I can't,' was Linda's reaction. She ran from other people's babies, especially from holding them. It took over a year to be able to work again with children in the Sunday school. It was the over-zealous Christians who were the worst. Linda told me, 'People would say, "God has a greater plan, and you can do more with the children at church," and I wanted to spit at them.'

With her head, Linda knew God was there, but in her

heart she asked him, 'Why?' She told him it wasn't fair –
why me? – and felt numb. She learned little from the
experiences, and is still not sure, several years later, that
she has come through. It will hit her, for example on holiday, when other couples have children with them, and
she will tell Paul again that it's not fair. 'But we have three
children in heaven,' he assures her. 'That's not the
same,' Linda replies. She fantasises sometimes, as if the
children are there at the table with her, the age they
would have been if they had lived, or she chats with them
in the car. She fears for Paul and herself in their old age,
and wonders who will look after them in the way they are
now caring for their parents. Even the Bible has brought
no comfort. It is all very sad.

So has any good come from this? A little, she would say,
but not much. Linda has recovered emotionally, and is
too busy to have children, with all her varied activities.
She has been able to care for a very sick relative and an
aging father, and does believe that God *is* good and faithful, and works out his plans. She also recalls the lady who
came to her in hospital and said with personal sorrow, 'At
least you could conceive.' Which brings me to a type of
bereavement which often fails to be recognised at all –
for the couple who cannot even start to dream of a
family.

Such are 'Wendy' and 'James'. Try as they would, they
could not start a family. Wendy went for all sorts of tests,
and no one came up with an answer – until James was
checked. Here was the difficulty – he had no sperm, nor
canals to carry it. They were heart-broken, though
strengthened in their love for each other. James survived
because at no time did Wendy accuse him, or say he was
'any less a man'. It was hard, however, to hear of school-
girl pregnancies and adulterous relationships that
resulted in a child when they, virgins at marriage, could

not have children. Friends avoided them, not knowing what to say. James says, 'It felt like having a death in the family but without a body to bury and therefore having no starting point from which to rebuild.' James asked God to heal him, even with people praying over him, but to no avail. Wendy became depressed, and they set a time-limit of eight months for prayer. At the end of that time, they accepted the verdict, though they do believe God could still work a miracle, if he so chose.

Their very positive attitude means that life is good, despite their hurt. Adoption is not an option, because James is now too old, but, as he says, 'We have each other, and therefore we have a family of two, and are content to stay that way if God so wishes.' As the wound heals, their pain has led them to a greater compassion for others who suffer grief and loss, and they know there is happiness, purpose and love beyond that grief. James takes strength from the courage of St Paul in prison, when he said, 'I have learned to be content whatever the circumstances' (Philippians 4:11). 'We are still learning,' James remarks, 'and there is now much more laughter and far fewer tears.'

Why have I gone into this sort of bereavement in such detail? Because, as I said at the beginning of this chapter, this was the one which, in all my meetings with people, caused the longest hurts. And because Ruth and I lost our only daughter through a miscarriage. The gap between our second and third sons is three years instead of the two between our first and second. This is due to Ruth miscarrying at four months. The only help we got was from a doctor who flatly informed Ruth she could not carry girls. Ruth felt there was something wrong with the baby, which helped her cope with losing it, but we never did have Sarah. Or perhaps we did and she's waiting for us. Talking with all these folk for this chapter, we have realised much more that we have had a real fifth child, and that is what is meant when the Bible says, 'Before I was born the Lord called me; from my birth he has made mention of my name' (Isaiah 49:1).

When a lady in our church said to Ruth that she herself had miscarried, another lady joined in the conversation, saying, 'How careless to lose a baby! We wouldn't do anything like that, would we Ruth?' Ruth was able to relate our loss, and how inadequate she had felt, and how she enjoys the visits of my sister's daughters, with pink on the washing line for a day or two!

We need to tell God of our sorrow, and release our dead baby, or our miscarried baby, to him. It might help to give the baby a name and, as a once-for-all, send love to that child via our heavenly Father. If the baby was intentionally aborted, the same could be done, asking God and the baby to forgive the wrong. 'You knit me together in my mother's womb' (Psalm 139:13); 'Before I formed you in the womb I knew you' (Jeremiah 1:5). Forgiving and forgetting will help us not to punish ourselves for ever. Let's be positive about it, and live our lives to the full, and let our grief give way to present joy and future hope.

6

A Verdict of Suicide . . .

'I can't tell you how awful that is when it happens in your family.' These words were the reply given by the former Lord Chancellor, Viscount Hailsham, when asked about the suicide of his half-brother, Edward. He spoke of an experience so many find hard to put into words.

Suicide is an especially difficult death to come to terms with, and yet I have been impressed with the very courageous and realistic way in which those with whom I have spoken have faced it, and it may be that their attitude will help others who have been similarly bereaved.

When I was a boy, I spied on an engaged couple! We had moved from Kent to Yorkshire when I was eight, and my parents invited Shirley and Geoff to come up and see us soon after the move. They had been two of the folk in a youth group my dad had run in Kent, and I was intrigued to have young love on view. I'm sure they didn't see me, but I saw them kissing in our bathroom – pretty sensational if you happen to be eight! They were so happy. Imagine our family shock when, some years later, we heard that Dad had been asked to go and speak at Geoff's funeral, because he had taken an overdose and died. Whatever had gone wrong? Recently I asked Shirley to tell me.

Geoff was a brilliant man, whose mind slowly fell apart.

Problems at work and a deteriorating mental illness led to several breakdowns and periods as an in-patient at a psychiatric hospital. In a marriage where everything had been shared, Geoff became aggressive and unable to communicate. He was off work and getting worse. Shirley said, 'It was hell with him in the house,' but he was frightened of returning to hospital. The situation became virtually untenable, with Geoff following Shirley everywhere round their home. She could not tell the doctor, or he would have sent Geoff to hospital. She found comfort in Christian friends, dreading to be alone with Geoff in the house.

As time went on, threats of suicide were made, including getting out knives to hurt himself. Each time Geoff had a breakdown he threatened to take an overdose. Shirley reached a point of desperation when she knelt on the bathroom floor, telling God she could take no more. Three days later, Geoff went to visit his vicar, who had arranged to pray with him. She never saw him again.

On reflection, Shirley realises Geoff must have been working things out for several days. After meeting the vicar, Geoff visited several chemists' shops to obtain small quantities of aspirin from each – he already had tranquillisers for his illness. When Shirley got home for lunch, he was not there. A phone call to the vicar led to the police being called in, and several friends being alerted. Where was Geoff? A huge search party found nothing. After a nightmare of a night Shirley felt Geoff must be at the church itself – and so it transpired, when their eighteen-year-old son Andrew found him lying dead in the loft of the church.

'I was absolutely shattered,' Shirley told me. The night he went missing, all the church leaders had come round to pray, and she had found comfort in their sensitivity, but the floodgates opened when he was found. It was such a traumatic death, and the problem of telling the children was the first requirement. As each child arrived home, Shirley spoke with them privately. Fearing for her fifteen-year-old daughter Judith, Shirley got Judith's best friend round to comfort her.

Such a death causes unusual hurts, including guilt and sorrow over what might have been and what was not done. Could more have been done? Could the death have been prevented? In Shirley's case, she genuinely feels she had given everything: Geoff's death was half expected. But there was a feeling of guilt over the unsaid 'sorrys' because of the atmospheres caused by the illness. She regrets the lack of communication, but how could she have got through to him? The police surgeon said that in his opinion Geoff's death was his ultimate act of love and courage, knowing what a burden he had become.

Shirley's bereavement had, in reality, begun years before, as the man she had loved slowly changed almost beyond recognition. Nevertheless, his death is one she has never really got over. At first she was shocked and numbed, hardly able to believe what had happened. She had fought and fought for Geoff to live, and now he was gone. She told the vicar she did not want to go to the funeral, and he replied that he didn't either – so they both went! The funeral proved to be good; a way of saying the 'goodbye' she had not said when he had walked up the road to the vicarage that fateful morning.

How has she got through? The first answer is – slowly. Shirley compares Geoff's death with that of her sister, who died of cancer. She and her husband had time to prepare, to choose the funeral hymns, to say their sorrys. With Geoff it was the opposite. As each of the children left home, the feelings of Geoff's going came back. Shirley still cannot go up to the church loft. Time has had to be a very slow healer, and her loss will always be there. The feeling of loneliness was the hardest. No one, not even children, can take the place of a partner, even for just talking together. The loss of a sexual relationship is particularly hard, and the adaptation to being single again.

Secondly, Shirley recovered through the tremendous support of family and friends. There were lots of prayers with the church fellowship, and the children got their act together wonderfully. Mike, then thirteen years old, remembered how Geoff used to bring Shirley a cup of tea in bed and fetch the paper. So Mike got on with these precious jobs instead. The children gave her space to shut herself in the bedroom to think, to cry, to grieve, to be exhausted, to be washed out, and to ask God why this had happened. Shirley was especially helped when, nine months later, the whole family agreed to a house move, and they were able to have a new beginning together.

And did God help? At first, he was the brunt of the inevitable recriminations: 'We gave our all to you, we tried to serve you, and now look what's happened.' Why was there no happy ending? The vicar was so shell-shocked, he himself had to receive counselling to enable him to counsel the family. It all seemed like a never-ending black tunnel, and hymns brought tears, not joy. But God never let go, and Shirley is so glad she was and is a Christian. She acknowledges that people who are not Christians do get through, but she is glad that she has faith, and has not lost it. Though she has hated people quoting: 'In all things God works for the good of those who love him' (Romans 8:28), she can see God's hand on her and the family. Many times she nearly gave up, but is now so thrilled they have come through. It was great to hear Shirley say that now she can't stop giving thanks to the Lord for all he has seen them through.

For me, the greatest testimony to Shirley and Geoff is to be seen in the lives of their children these many years since his death in 1976. Each is involved in Christian work of one form or another, and the thirteen-year-old Mike is now a full-time evangelist with me in the 40:3 Trust. His dad's death inevitably had a huge impact on his life. He knew Geoff was ill, even to the extent of restraining him on one occasion from taking a knife out of a drawer. He is grateful for the love and support others gave after the death. How does he view what happened? 'Suicide's a cruel word,' he says. 'I believe God called him home. He wasn't being heartless and selfish. The Coroner was right when he said it was an act of love towards the family.'

There are 'if onlys' – if only Geoff had said, 'I love you,' as his last words. But Mike grew up quickly, and has no resentment. 'Dad is in heaven, and better off there.' My own father, who spoke at the funeral, feels the same. Geoff is happy in heaven. Before Geoff's death, my father would say that no Christian could commit suicide. Now he recalls how this fine man was buffeted by life, and how badly hurt his mind was. Geoff did not turn his back on Christ. It is not for us to sit in judgement on the rights and wrongs. 'You, then, why do you judge your brother? Or why do you look down on your brother? For we will all stand before God's judgment seat' (Romans 14:10).

If we are not to stand in judgement over a suicide victim, we ought to adopt a similar approach to ourselves. The question is bound to be asked, 'What have I done wrong to cause this?' Likewise, regrets such as, 'If only I had . . . ' or, 'If only they had . . . ' spring up. We are left to carry another's guilt. My sister, Sue, a trained counsellor herself, had a client who committed suicide. Sue was devastated, but her supervisor told her, 'We're all adults. Don't take their actions on yourself – they chose to do that.'

In coming to terms with a bereavement of this sort, we must try to draw out what is positive. Self-blame should be avoided, and time can move us on as we reinvest in the future. If there are big questions, we need a mature, stable friend (one trained in counselling is best) to talk to. Or you might like to try a little role-play: put yourself opposite an empty chair and imagine your dead relative or friend is actually in the chair. Talk to them, saying and asking whatever you want. Ask them why they did it, and tell them what you have been left with. Share your feeling of guilt, and your anger and hurts. Then cross over and sit in the empty chair, and be the person you have spoken to. Give the answers as if you were them – you will be sur- prised at what they will say! Finally, go back and receive the answers. It is a method of help called the 'Gestalt Empty Chair' and may help resolve many unspoken issues.

Above all, we must not break apart ourselves. In such a deep hurt, God does not want us to be shattered. It was said of Jesus, 'A bruised reed he will not break, and a smouldering wick he will not snuff out' (Matthew 12:20). Death is always horrendous, so let us not make it more difficult. If we are not the bereaved, but the helpers, we need to listen to the bereaved as they pour out their pain and grief. We must be unshockable as we simply care. Before Jesus died on the cross, Isaiah said this about him: 'Surely he took up our infirmities and carried our sor- rows . . . he was pierced for our transgressions, he was crushed for our iniquities; the punishment that brought us peace was upon him, and by his wounds we are healed' (Isaiah 53:4–5). If we have been wrong in any way, God's forgiveness is there to be accepted. If we have been hurt, we can receive his healing.

This healing is so important, because a suicide death is one we think will never happen to someone we know.

When Nathan took his own life, that was Tina's reaction. Tina had known Nathan for over five years before he died, and had been married to him for three-and-a-half of those. He had always been ill throughout their relationship, and this eventually led to severe depression. With two very small children, Tina tried to stand with Nathan as he struggled to face each day. For weeks before he died, Nathan was suicidal, and Tina never knew if he would come home from work. Prescribed heavy anti-depressant drugs by both the psychiatrist at the hospital and his own doctor, he had all he needed to take an over-dose. After visiting her mother one day, Tina came home to find Nathan dead.

With two babies, life had to go on. Tina's 'if onlys' were for the doctors, giving him so many pills and not finding any other solution than to tell Nathan, 'You're depressed.' For fifteen months after his death she did not feel like crying, and had to be independent. Then it all got to her – grieving happens when it does. Church was her place for tears and she cried every time she went. This crying to God helped a great deal through really low times, and Tina is glad God knows her so well. As she has been able to throw herself at God, she has experienced the truth of his promise: 'He heals the broken-hearted and binds up their wounds' (Psalm 147:3). But, as she told me, 'You just don't imagine it can happen to you.' Nathan was twenty-three.

Such seems to be the common reaction to a suicide death. People speak of a 'terrible waste', and of wasted lives. Yet investigations show this to be a serious malaise in our society: for example, it is estimated that one in a hundred fifteen- to nineteen-year-old females attempts suicide in any one year. Loneliness, isolation, depression, failure (or, at least, failure to come up to perceived expectations), grieving, missing a dead relative or friend, broken relationships, lack of communication – so many reasons are given. And so much pain and anguish result.

There are bound to be recriminations. If we feel guilty because of someone's suicide, we should not sweep our guilt away or try to justify ourselves. No doubt we could have done better. But we must give our sense of failure to a loving God, who longs to forgive us. He will pick us up, as we find from him that he is the one who really can put us right again. Of all the chapters on bereavement through someone actually dying, this is bound to be the 'messy' one. There will be lots of loose ends. We may ask, 'Should I have picked up the signs?' If the suicide victim was younger, parents especially will feel they have failed as parents. If the person threatened it would happen, we will wish we had acted to prevent what then caused the death. Big questions often arise about the rottenness of the world, and of a society which seems unwilling to care, or unable to help.

But, at the end of all the questions and confusion and guilt, only God knows the whole. When Jesus died on the cross, it was to carry our sorrow and to pay for our wrong. In the mystery of it all, we must accept the lovely comment of St Paul: 'Your life is now hidden with Christ in God' (Colossians 3:3). In that great gulf of failure and inadequacy, God understands, forgives and carries us on. Let's allow him to do it.

7

'He Had no Faith'

One of the greatest comforts in any bereavement is when we know for sure that the person who has died has gone 'home' to heaven. That is why there are people who refuse to use the word 'died', preferring to say that their loved one has 'passed over', 'passed on', 'gone before', 'gone to glory', 'fallen asleep in Jesus' – or some similar expression of hope. It is all very soothing. Which makes the death of someone who does not come within this category all the harder to face, and the grieving more agonising.

Let's dare to face this one, and see if there is any consolation to be had in the case of someone who, as far as anyone can tell, had no faith. As a first port of call, I talked with my father, who for over twenty-five years was Town Clerk of Harrogate in Yorkshire and, as such, had close dealings with people coming from all sorts of religious standpoints, some of them having little or no belief at all. How did my father feel as he attended many funerals of those about whom it was said, 'He had no faith'?

One such funeral was that of a member of the local authority with whom my father had had very close dealings over several years. 'Bill' was definitely not a Christian. He was a great drinker, and my father's tee-total stance amused him, as did his reputation as a 'Bible thumper'! Despite their being poles apart spiritually, a deep friendship developed, and not a little respect for one another. Bill would joke about Dad's non-drinking, and Dad would have a go at Bill for being a hypocrite and singing hymns at civic services. 'Well, they seem to do people good,' said Bill, 'so I'm helping them as I sing!'

The night before he died of cancer of the liver (not helped by a lifetime of over-drinking), Bill said that he'd 'have a glass of Neville Knox's brew'! Who knows what he was thinking at the end, this man who had accepted a Gideons' Gospel from Dad, and was happy to talk about God and faith in him? Perhaps he never really saw what Christianity was all about. Dad lost a good friend when Bill died. Has he lost him for ever? 'I don't know,' is Dad's answer. 'It's between him and God.' Dad is helped by some words of Jesus in John 9. A blind man had been brought to Jesus, and Jesus switched the situation to talk about spiritual blindness: whether people can see and know God and his love. The religious leaders asked if they were 'blind' in this way, and Jesus gave a telling reply: 'If you were blind, you would not be guilty of sin; but now that you claim you can see, your guilt remains' (John 9:41). Only God and the person concerned truly know if that person has had the ability, the insight and the opportunity to respond to God's claim on their life. That is why Dad cannot despair about Bill, though he cannot be sure, either.

In such circumstances, I always recall a remarkable incident at the beginning of the Bible. Abraham had been told by God that the cities of Sodom and Gomorrah would be destroyed. Thousands of years after the event, the names of those cities live on as being synonymous with all that is evil. Yet, despite their wickedness, Abraham pleaded with God to spare both cities for the sake of the good people in them, and said a great thing to God in his prayer: 'Far be it from you to do such a thing – to kill the righteous with the wicked, treating the righteous and the wicked alike. Far be it from you! Will not the Judge of all the earth do right?' (Genesis 18:25). And that must be correct: God will do what is right by every person who dies. He is the Judge, not us. After all, *we* never know, not for sure.

Dick was another with whom Dad had dealings, and he proved that a death-bed turning to God is always possible. Dad was the Civil Defence Controller for the Harrogate district, and Dick was his Civil Defence Officer. A most decent man, Dick talked with Dad in his office about Dad's faith, but did nothing about having a faith of his own. One night Dad went to visit Dick as he lay dying, coincidentally like Bill, of cancer of the liver. My father again shared God's love with Dick, and how he could trust his life to Jesus Christ. Dick admitted that he had not prayed in forty years, but he did that night. He asked to be ready to meet God, and three days later he did. As Dad put it, Dick was Dad's watchman as Civil Defence Officer, and Dad was Dick's watchman as a Christian. Unless Dad had told everyone at the funeral of Dick's turning to God, no one else would have known. How many others come this late? If we are grieving for someone, it is not for us to know with absolute certainty that that person is away from God.

At times like this the safest way is to look to the grace of God, and not to act as judge and jury. Such was, and is, the approach of 'James', as he remembers his sister 'Esther'. Brought up with no real faith, Esther was willing to change her religion to marry. Terrified as a youngster by a frightening experience after playing with a ouija board, she immersed herself in art, becoming brilliant at her subject. Then a dreadful wasting illness slowly crippled her, eventually leading to her death. Meanwhile,

James had become a Christian, and joyfully told his sister. Esther indulged him, but was also very much against this step and alternated between being over-kind and over-critical. As time went on, her attitude hardened, and her Christian nurse was the butt of many a joke. With the increase of her illness, Esther became even more vehement as she totally rejected all James now loved. The illness left James with only memories of a better past, and Esther's death was a relief.

Inevitably, James hates the idea that Esther is somehow not now in God's kingdom. The Christian nurse has told him that she believes Esther is with God, but James can only hope. Though people say he did his best, he feels he could and should have done more, especially in spending more time with Esther, and he has no excuse for not visiting, despite her strong opposition to his faith. He did challenge her directly, as did the nurse, and he knows God would not shut his sister out just because of his own inadequacies.

James has learned two excellent things from this terrible bereavement. First, it is now God's problem, not his. He must leave Esther to God's grace, and not for ever live with a sense of blame, as he lets God forgive the failure he feels (rightly or wrongly). In the second place, he now has a greater sense of urgency in sharing his Christian faith with others who need to hear. All this is tied in with a natural grief at Esther's death, particularly after seeing such a vital and loving sister slowly fade away. He misses her terribly.

I hope James draws some comfort from a spectacular last-minute conversion experienced by the most unlikely of people, related in the Bible in Luke 23. When Jesus was crucified, two criminals were also being similarly put to death. As all three hung there slowly dying, one of the men turned to Jesus and admitted he had done wrong.

He then said, 'Jesus, remember me when you come into your kingdom,' to which Jesus replied, 'Today you will be with me in paradise' (Luke 23:43). The man could not have left his cry a moment longer, nor could he have received a more generous response. Occasionally there is a 'death-bed conversion'. We should never presume on it for ourselves, but we should never despair of it for others.

Like my father with Dick, I also have been with a man near death who has realised his need of a heart relationship with God, and has turned to him in time. It can and does happen, and our knowledge of someone's eternal destiny is limited on most occasions, unless we know they really were Christians before they died. I do accept that there is no record of the criminal on the third cross repenting, and that there are those who are away from God for ever. I regret that very much, which is one reason why I work as an evangelist, to bring the good news to people so that they can meet Jesus in time.

In so doing, I am merely carrying on what Jesus started. Of all people, he knew that mankind was away from God because mankind had so chosen. Jesus said that he had come 'to seek and to save what was lost' (Luke 19:10). Christians are deeply concerned to help others to come back to God. Their greatest hurt is when someone apparently refuses to accept God's love, especially if it is too late to do anything.

Such is Betty's feeling about her husband. She was involved in the church, and he was happy for her to be so, attending various events with her. Neither had any real faith; nor did the rest of her family. Three heart attacks following quickly one after the other, and her husband was dead.

It was not till some years later that Betty realised that for Christianity to be real it had to be personal. She entrusted her life to Jesus Christ, asking him to forgive her for what she had done wrong in her life and stay with her for ever. It was then that the obvious question arose: What had happened to her husband, her father and mother and other family members who, as far as she knew, had died without any relationship with God? Before she had become a Christian it had not bothered her, and she had assumed her husband had gone to heaven. I asked Betty how she felt, and how she had come to terms with her dilemma.

In asking others, she had discovered it was a very grey, unclear area, and it remains so in her own mind. Because the minister of her church would visit her husband in hospital before he died, she does not know all that happened in his mind. There can be no personal sense of guilt, as Betty was in no position to say or do anything herself. She has done the best thing, and ultimately the only thing, she could: she has given the dilemma over to God and received his peace in her heart. Such peace cannot be invented, nor can she get rid of her worry by herself. She has turned to Jesus, who has said, 'Peace I leave with you; my peace I give you. I do not give to you as the world gives. Do not let your hearts be troubled and do not be afraid' (John 14:27). Betty's concern now is for those she can still speak to, and she is glad to have a real faith to share. As she retraces her memories of her husband, Betty takes comfort in those most famous words of David: 'Even though I walk through the valley of the shadow of death, I will fear no evil, for you are with me; your rod and your staff, they comfort me' (Psalm 23:4).

As a further help on this very tricky subject, I went to see two friends of mine who are church ministers, to ask them how they deal with the funerals of those who seemingly died without any faith in God. The Revd Tony Holmes is a long-time friend, and he aims to be as positive as possible. He is not prepared to say what he does not know to be true, as people expect honesty. If he believes 'John' has gone to heaven, he says it, and if he doesn't know, he doesn't say. But, as Tony does not know of John's last moments, he equally cannot and will not say John is not with God. 'Most people come to the conclusion,' says Tony, 'that they hope that in his last hours John did make his peace with God.'

Tony is particularly concerned with the grief of those who loved John, so his aim in a funeral service, and in counselling the bereaved, is to thank God for the good things in John's life; for the happy times, the positive memories. There needs to be joy mingled with the sorrow, as people remember the way John related to them. At such a time, those who mourn John can come to a living faith in the God whose own Son died on the cross.

My own minister, The Revd Dr Rod Allon-Smith, adopts a similar approach. If Rod were to take the funeral of 'Joe', he would try to weave in three strands to the service. First, he would speak of the grief and sadness which need to be faced and acknowledged, and lived through. Secondly, he would want to give thanks for Joe's life, however dreadful he had been! Finally, Rod would speak of our Christian hope. This last strand is not based on who Joe was, but in who Jesus is, and on his dying and rising again. Rod delights in talking about the character of God, because we can trust him and his right judgement. He leaves the question hanging as to where Joe has gone, unless he is sure Joe was a Christian. Like Tony, Rod is not going to give false hope: 'I'm sure Joe is with Jesus now.' But neither is he going to condemn Joe to hell, because that would be Rod passing judgement, and it is not for him to do that. Such a course would act like a curse on Joe's widow and family, and be a barrier between them and God.

Rod reminded me of the lovely words used at funerals,

as we say to God, 'We entrust Joe to your faithful keeping, in the faith of Jesus Christ, who died and rose again to save us.' When we commend Joe to our heavenly Father, we are not making assumptions as to what is happening to him, and God does not have to accept our commendation. But we have done what we can, and we have expressed our own faith in Jesus. In a similar way, people often ask me how I was able to defend people I 'knew' to be guilty when I was a solicitor. My reply is always the same: I only knew someone to be guilty if they told me they were. If I did not know, then it was my duty to speak on their behalf in court, not to pre-judge the issue in my office. If eventually they were found guilty, that was not my verdict.

One final word of comfort for those who are bereaved of someone they love, and are not sure if they have gone to heaven (and even if they are almost certain they have not). A great friend of mine, George Green, often quotes the first verse of a hymn by Joseph Parker, which I find an encouragement and help:

> God holds the key of all unknown
> And I am glad.
> If other hands should hold the key,
> Or if he trusted it to me,
> I might be sad.

8

The Budgie's Dead

Is this some kind of joke? When a special person dies, that is bereavement. Who cares if some animal dies? This cannot be a chapter about dogs and cats – and budgerigars – can it?

Yes it can, and yes it is. People can be deeply heart-broken when a pet dies, and it is no laughing matter. It may be a problem peculiar to certain cultures, but I have found that the bereavement felt at the death of an animal is very real, and often long-lasting. More than once the question has arisen as to where the pet has gone, and, in extreme cases, one hears something along the lines of, 'If my dog won't be in heaven, I don't want to go myself.' If you feel bereaved of a much-loved pet, have no fear. I am about to treat this chapter seriously.

We had to face this sort of loss in our own family when our budgerigar died. I say 'our', but he was really David's, and David was the one who grieved. Penny, our dog, was around when David was born, so she was the family pet, but Peter came as David's own special little friend when he was seven. David had such fun with Peter, especially when Peter's beak changed colour and 'he' had to be renamed Petra! What is it about a pet that gets to you? Peter/Petra had such character, and was often the refuge in the storm, a safe confidant and a cheery voice in a rough old world.

One morning we came downstairs and he was dead, a little bundle of yellow and green feathers lying on the floor of the cage, not breathing. Poor David! Eighteen months of fun and laughter, and now this. After school we took Peter down to the bottom of the garden and buried him under the trees, where robins would sing, and where tears could be shed quietly. We thanked God for giving us Peter, and for his making us happy, and we asked God to help us in our sadness. It's all very real when you are eight. David is no fool, and he knows that any pet is bound to die in the nature of things. But it does not stop sorrow, nor a continuing feeling of loss. David hopes to see Peter in heaven, and is glad God did help him feel better as he prayed.

But little boys aren't the only ones who get hurt. My mother-in-law, Joyce, is a great dog-lover, and has had nine in all as pets. Yet the one she remembers most is the one who was her age. Joyce and her puppy Bob grew up together for eight years – baby and puppy into a girl and her dog. Bob was a bit of a lad, as well as a great companion, and he went off to do a bit of courting from time to time. One day, on such an outing, someone gave him strychnine, and Joyce watched him die, slowly, in two days of agony. It was the first time she had ever seen an adult cry, when her mother wept, and the shock meant there was never another dog in the house. Joyce determined she would have a dog when she had her own home, hence the eight others to make up the nine in all. But Bob is still the most remembered, and time alone healed her bereavement. In her seventies, the memories are still as fresh as if it were yesterday.

Surely, though, an adult in a similar situation to David and Joyce will cope better? Not so, it would seem. My local paper recently carried an article nearly half a page long on one of the regular columnists having just been to the vet for her fourteen-year-old dog to be put down. She related how she had cried, and bid him farewell with words of love. The article was written with real emotion and seriousness, and will have been read in the same way. Whatever age you are, the death of your pet will almost certainly hurt you deeply, and it will take time to get over.

My sister Sue had a beautiful golden retriever called Sheba. Sheba was everyone's friend, and was, as many animals are, a silent counsellor. If Sue, or one of Sue's friends, had an unresolved problem, or a hurt, Sheba had the answer. You would simply put Sheba on the lead and go for a long walk round the park to talk things through with a dog who would listen, wag her tail and not give you stupid answers. A hug with Sheba told you life could go on, people could be forgiven, there was a way through and supper was waiting! And if you wanted to be a teeny bit naughty, Sheba would do it for you: every photo Sue has of Sheba is of her misbehaving, as she wrecked another flower bed, or climbed out of another smelly pond.

At fifteen, Sheba got cancer and was in great pain. The kindest thing you can do for a loved pet is to put it out of its misery, so Sue and her husband Derek took Sheba to the vet for the inevitable. Sheba wagged her tail at seeing her old friend the vet, who promptly burst into tears, along with Sue and Derek! Sue told me that before Sheba died, she thought that people who grieved over animals were mad. But not any more. Years later, Sheba is still missed around the house, and Derek will not drive past the vet's surgery. Now Sue is able to cry with others who lose their pets, and tell them she knows how they are feeling.

This sense of bereavement at the death of an animal is often the worse because, however right the reason, the pet owner is responsible for the death, when the animal has to be put down. The decision itself causes agony, however necessary. When I talked with Audrey, that was part of her hurt. One Christmas she was given a beautiful Dalmatian puppy, and for the next ten years they were the closest of friends. Then terrible arthritis set in, and many injections failed to help. After a weekend away, Audrey collected her dog from a neighbour, and it was clear the future was bleak. Should the dog be put down, or allowed to die in slow pain? Both dog and mistress knew why they were going to the vet's, and Audrey stayed till the end. 'But when the head went down, I fled,' she said.

Dreadful grief followed until, two days later, a most remarkable thing happened. Sitting alone in a sunlit lounge, Audrey saw her Dalmatian walk in, in the very best of health. She looked at Audrey as if to say, 'I'm all right now. There's no need to mourn.' And at that moment, she disappeared. Audrey has never grieved bitterly again, though she felt unable to have another dog for over five years, and it was thirteen years afterwards when she told me, and her eyes were filled with tears. But Audrey feels that God used this dramatic vision to let her know that all was well, especially after her horrendous decision to hasten her dog's death.

I have thought long and hard about Audrey seeing her dog two days after the dog had died. I do not doubt for a moment that it happened – Audrey is a very level-headed lady, and there is no reason for her making up such a story. It does take time to adjust between death and separation. There are many examples of a bereaved person sensing the dead one as 'being there', even to the point of feeling an arm round them, or smelling their perfume or after-shave.

Experts will explain this by saying that the unconscious mind refuses to believe that the death has happened, and so manufactures this sort of 'appearance' or feeling in a desperate attempt to convince the more conscious part of the mind that the loved one is really alive and there. What the bereaved needs is help in letting go.

Perhaps it happened like that for Audrey. Whatever, I have no doubt that she reported a genuine experience. If she needed help in 'letting go', the appearance did that, without a doubt. Above all, Audrey felt good about it, and there was a sense of God's peace, enabling her to feel released from her 'tie' with her dog and closer to God. Is it beyond belief to see God's hand in the whole incident? I don't think it feels wrong. If nothing like this has ever happened to you, don't will it. But, if it has, feel good about it, and move on from there to the release it brings.

Dogs have featured prominently thus far, and they are allegedly man's best friend, but cats can be important friends, too, and sorely missed after their death. My friends Hazel and Fred would agree with that. Their great joy was Tucker. To begin with they were not greatly enamoured with the idea of having him. Indeed, Hazel used to find her hands went numb whenever she picked up a cat. But their church minister said he had two cats, and one of them would have to be put down as no home could be found for him. So Tucker moved in with Hazel and Fred, and became part of their lives, almost like the child they never had. People said he ruled their lives!

Tucker was big and black, and quite a character. His wonderful temperament meant he never scratched, or bit. But perhaps the pampering he received meant he never needed to! Throughout his seventeen years he was never put out at night, and Fred would sometimes wait up till one or two in the morning for Tucker to come in. Faddy with his food, he disdained tins and was fed on fresh rabbit and fish. Life went on, year after year, with Tucker running the show, till he started to fade away. Age and illness led to a series of injections, but there came a time when he was unable to eat. The vet had no desire to put him down, but Tucker took to his bed.

One Saturday night, he wandered into the bedroom and put his claw on Hazel's hand, as if to say, 'Please do something.' It was his goodbye. Weeping and agitated, Hazel called the vet, who admitted that he personally could not put an old friend down, and made his assistant do it! Hazel and Fred walked out with an empty basket. The basket has recently been filled by Susie, but there will never be another Tucker, and they have not got over his death, though it was some years ago. Will they see Tucker again? Hazel is not so sure, but Fred feels they will. Both have known God's comfort, but they have needed to grieve, and there is a deep sense of loss.

How, then, are we supposed to cope when a beloved pet dies? Be it a horse or a hamster, a parrot or a python, others may think we are silly for mourning its death, but the bereavement is felt anyway. Hazel told me she needed to grieve, and she would only have harmed herself if she had failed to. Let's be realistic about our loss: almost all birds and animals have a much shorter lifespan than humans, and our pet was bound to die in what seems a short time to us but may have been quite a long life for them.

We can find the photos of our pet which remind us of the happy and crazy times we shared – the 'best budgie competition' when ours came last, the adventure when the cat got stuck up the tree, the scream of Aunt Flo as she met our stick insect, the dog-and-the-snowman scene – and we can be grateful for happiness shared. We should never try to replace our dead friend, but we can get another pet to create new joys. And, as in any bereavement, God wants the chance to wrap us in his love, and heal the pain in our hearts.

Which leads to the hardest question of all: Will we see our animal friend again? If we could understand how brilliant heaven will be, many of our questions would fade into insignificance, but 'no eye has seen, no ear has heard, no mind has conceived what God has prepared for those who love him' (1 Corinthians 2:9). We will be part of a new creation, with new bodies, where we 'will reign for ever and ever' (Revelation 22:5).

Will animals be there? When we look at the first chapter of the Bible, the whole of God's creation is described as being 'good', and that included all things living, with animals and birds prominent within this description. It would seem odd for the splendour of the present creation to be totally scrapped. However, I believe there is a more positive answer. In Isaiah 11, God speaks of the kingdom which Jesus will bring in, and these promises are included:

> The wolf will live with the lamb, the leopard will lie down with the goat, the calf and the lion and the yearling together; and a little child will lead them. The cow will feed with the bear, their young will lie down together, and the lion will eat straw like the ox. The infant will play near the hole of the cobra, and the young child put his hand into the viper's nest. They will neither harm nor destroy on all my holy mountain, for the earth will be full of the knowledge of the Lord as the waters cover the sea (Isaiah 11:6–9).

These words, echoed again in Isaiah 65:25, speak of a time which clearly has not happened yet, nor will it till the return of Jesus Christ to this earth. If you like animals, they will be around. If you don't like them now, they will be much more fun later! Whether your particular animal will be there is a question which can only honestly be answered with: 'I don't know.' I like what my minister said to one of his children. A little pet was receiving a private burial – just minister and child present – and he was asked if the pet was going to heaven. 'I don't know if we'll see it,' my minister said, 'but we'll give it to Jesus, and he'll decide.'

One thing's for sure: when Jesus said that his Father sees each sparrow which falls to the ground (Matthew 10:29), it shows God's care for all the animal kingdom. He cares that our pets have died, and he cares for us in our very real bereavement. We must let his care fill our hearts with his love and hope. Here's a happy thought: W.M. Letts says this in his 'Songs of Leinster':

So I laugh when I hear them make it plain
That dogs and men never meet again.
For all their talk who'd listen to them,
With the soul in the shining eyes of him?
Would God be wasting a dog like Tim?

PART TWO

Bereaved by Life

9

A Child Leaves

'Goodbye, my son.'

How does a parent feel when a child leaves home? In January 1992 I found out. In so doing, I also realised in a more powerful way than ever before that the word 'bereavement' does not just mean losing through a death, but also having someone, or something, taken from you by the natural course of life.

For all our faults, we are a happy family. With four sons (and no daughters!) there is rarely a dull moment. A family of six can have brilliant times without much outside help, even though we all have lots of friends and relatives we see frequently. Each of our boys has been reasonably sporty, with the oldest two reaching County level at rugby football; and music has featured prominently also. Thus there is always lots going on, and much to share together.

In the summer of 1991 our eldest son, Matthew, swept up nine 'A' grade GCSE passes, and the future looked rosy. By then, Matthew had shown a real interest in pursuing a particular career for which specialist training was needed, which could best be obtained at a residential sixth form college about ninety miles from our home. After a series of difficult interviews, he was successful in gaining a place, starting in January 1992. The whole family was delighted for him, and the Christmas holidays were taken up with preparation and packing.

I remember once having a minor operation under general anaesthetic. I had plans to jump out of bed afterwards and rush straight back to work, and I now recall the feeling of shock as I realised I was as weak as a kitten, and I took ages to recover. This is the nearest experience I have had to help me try to explain what happened next with Matthew, because my planned reaction and my actual reaction were so different. In my head I knew that Matthew, as with each son, would one day leave home. He couldn't stay with us for ever! Even if he'd waited till he got married, my Bible told me that 'a man will leave his father and mother and be united to his wife' (Genesis 2:24). I had left home well before I got married, and though the first weeks had been lonely, I knew it was right. And so it was now for Matthew.

Alas, there was some distance between my head and my heart, and my heart failed to listen to the logic and intelligence of my brave theories. As with my operation, I was amazed by my reaction, because I realised I was bereaved by Matthew's leaving. For him I was delighted: he had done so well, his future was bright, and here was a young man with life opening up. But for me, I was bereft. Perhaps it had something to do with my own nomadic lifestyle as an itinerant evangelist, going away frequently for missions and other speaking events, and needing a stable home to return to. Maybe I had made my family my friends and failed to build a network of other close friends too. I felt that one of my very best friends had gone; that one of my most special people had left. Our family life would never be the same. As time has passed, I know now I was taking too extreme a view; our togetherness does not need to rely on a continual physical presence, and our love crosses the miles. Learning that lesson was hard, and there were times of heartache and tears.

One such moment occurred a fortnight after Matthew's departure when the rest of us were at our church. It was one of those rare occasions when I was not helping with the service, or preaching elsewhere. Sitting with my wife, each of our other boys was involved in their own activity in the church, and I was deeply conscious that we were 'one short'. In a moving communion service, all my love for my son and my loneliness without him welled up. As I received bread and wine at the communion rail I began to cry, and was unable to stop. Others came and went, but I remained kneeling there, tears flowing freely. 'Can I pray for you?' asked the vicar. 'No, I'm fine,' I replied, and I was. I was weeping with a Father who had said 'goodbye' to his Son as he had left heaven to come to our world, and he understood. As the last person came to the rail I dried my eyes and was able to return to my seat, knowing God's love and understanding. I still miss Matthew each time he leaves to go to his new life, and I guess I always will. But God has met me in my need, and he has my son in his care.

It was Kahil Gilbran who said, 'Love knows not its own depth until the hour of separation.' I am glad I have discovered how much I love my children through the leaving of the eldest. I am also pleased to say that my reaction was by far the most extreme of all the family. My wife, Ruth, was much more mature and philosophical. She was happy to see him go. She had thought things through much better than I. She had always vowed, when we had children, that they would make their own lives, and they would be their own people, not hers. Equally, each child would always be welcome back. What Ruth missed most was Matthew's presence round the house, and the lack of huge piles of laundry. The milk bill was remarkably lower too! Ruth remembered how her gran had said to her mum, 'If you want to keep a child, you've got to let it go,' and this is what Ruth did with Matthew. But there is always time to write a daily letter to keep news and assurances of love and support flowing to him. This also helps Ruth to feel close to him. However, she is not sure how she will face the last son's day of departure. . . .

Perhaps our weakness was in having boys: would it have been easier if our eldest had been a girl? My friends Clare and Mike would definitely say not. Their family life was especially important, because both of them had become Christians after their three daughters were born, and thus to have a Christian home was extremely precious, and the family was and is very closely knit. At eighteen, Sara was off to university to study art history. Now on the threshold of her own independent life, she looked forward to leaving. Mike and Clare prepared her for the problems, having done the same themselves in their time, and they also planned with the other two girls for more bedroom space and the other changes there would be. But they never prepared themselves as a couple, or as parents.

A child leaving means busy times beforehand, and therefore little thinking time. It did not register that a hole would be left when Sara got on the train. Having to get up at 5am for the train did not help and, as Sara disappeared from view, Clare and Mike could not look at each other. Nor were they able at that stage to console one another. Back at home Clare poured her heart out to God, and wept and wept. She felt as if she had been kicked in the stomach and was very depressed, unable to give Sara to God from her heart. Mike was quite unprepared for how low he would feel, and found the physical separation hardest, not having Sara around. He did not feel he could hand the whole situation over to God to make it right. It is at times like these that a Christian community needs to swing into action, and that is what happened. Many prayers were offered, love poured in and practical support included Clare having lunch with a friend that first day. 'I don't know how people cope who don't have that,' says Clare.

,A reassuring phone call with Sara that night enabled Clare and Mike to draw together and console each other. After a few days, Sara was reporting that she was doing well, and they realised how fortunate they were. Going up after half-term to see her room was another part of the healing process, as was seeing Sara's confidence as a student. As time went by, Clare was able to hand Sara over to God's care. She told me a lovely thing: the distance ceased to be a problem when she felt able to send her love to Sara via God! Each new term is a new wrench, but Clare copes better than Mike – the strength of a woman! But God has been allowed to grip the situation, and that is their greatest help.

We dads do seem to be a gang of softies, I'm afraid, because Tony and Judy's story is not dissimilar to Mike and Clare's. You will recall Tony and Judy as the parents of baby Mark in Chapter 5. They had three daughters after Mark's death, and called the eldest Deborah. Like Sara, Debbie got the exams she needed to go to the college of her choice to study the speech sciences she needed to become a speech therapist. Here was her opportunity, and Judy was delighted to see her daughter growing up, entering a new period of womanhood. Having been to college herself, she knew how Debbie needed that freedom and sense of responsibility, away from Mum's control. Tony simply hated the idea of her going, though he was delighted she had done so well, and had got in to college.

As they parted at the door of Debbie's room at college, they clung to each other. That in itself was positive rather than negative, for it showed that Debbie cared: how much worse a couldn't-care-less attitude would have been. Tony felt lost, full of fatherly concern for a daughter, protective instincts to the fore as she faced a hard world. But as he and Judy put Debbie prayerfully into God's hands, he realised that God would care. The toughest thing was letting Debbie be on her own, for that would be proof positive whether or not their Christian parenting counted for anything. It did, and now Debbie has been able to take her own stand with a faith which is her own, not just shared within a safe Christian family. God thus proves himself again to Judy and Tony, and Debbie shows them she is not their little girl any more. That is a very hard lesson for any parent.

Sometimes it is a hard lesson for a child too, and a kick out of the nest may be needed! When a child leaves in those circumstances, bereavement is all but non-existent. I was glad to talk with Geoff and Sylvia, because their son Richard left with their planning, their preparation and their push. Both Geoff and Sylvia had been glad to leave their own childhood homes when their time had come, and were determined to enable their own family to move forward to independent adulthood. When Richard, at eighteen, dropped any ideas of moving away they were surprised, and they decided he was not going to have cheap digs with them for ever. Eventually they helped him find somewhere else to live, and there was no feeling of loss at all. Now married, and living in the next town, his leaving has worked well for all of them, and relationships are excellent. Careful planning, and an understanding of a child's needs to be an adult, may obviate any grieving and solve this sort of bereavement before it ever arises.

Surprisingly, when Geoff and Sylvia's daughter left home they both felt a huge sense of bereavement. Kathryn planned a year out before going to university.

The same thinking was obviously there as for Richard, and the same planning and preparation. Yet they felt dreadful. Perhaps it was simply because she went so far away and for so long, as she spent a year in the West Indies, with no phone contact and only one visit throughout the time. Or it could have been because they had experienced a difficult year before she went. Was it because she chose to go, rather than them choosing for Richard to leave? Whatever the reason, Sylvia's sleep was affected, and Kathryn's loneliness and misery at being so far away was shared at home, where both Sylvia and Geoff felt so helpless.

This seems to be one of the great difficulties in this type of bereavement. Parents are able to use all their strength and experience when a child has problems at home, thus having to let that child fend for him or herself, all alone, is a great burden on the parents, who cannot do what they have always done up to that point. Lack of news adds to the hurt, and waiting a fortnight for Kathryn's first letter was painful. Sylvia and Geoff were able to speak with a parent of a girl who had already been on a similar venture, and that helped to reassure them: sharing problems can provide a support. Being able to do something, rather than sit wondering, is a way through, so the sending of letters, photos, news cuttings and supplies can enable parents like Sylvia and Geoff to feel they have a part in their daughter's life. Even one visit during a long absence will make life much more bearable, as they found by going to Jamaica for a brief stay.

For Geoff and Sylvia, there were two special helps. Prayer spanned the miles, and Geoff felt that God would be with Kathryn even when he could not. Sylvia was comforted by the way Kathryn showed she had a faith of her own, and that God was using this experience to further Kathryn's life. The other very special help was in a most moving letter, written by Kathryn and left in her room for her parents to find after her departure. In it, she wrote of her love for them, her thanks for all they had done and her belief that God would care for them all. Needless to say, Sylvia and Geoff fell apart as they read it, but at the same time they were comforted by her thoughtfulness.

There are two particular circumstances in which a parent will feel more deeply a child's leaving. The first is when the child is the last to go (as my wife said, that is the one she fears). When Chris's son Simon left home, she felt pride, excitement and a sadness swallowed up in sharing his exploits. But when her other child, daughter Rebecca, went to university, the house was left empty save for husband Alan. There was still the pride and excitement, and the sharing. But there was also loneliness, with no one to come home to after a day's teaching. Above all, there was a loss of purpose as Chris's function as a mother seemed to have come to an end, and she felt no longer needed. Even worse, she felt old, and that life would be downhill from now on. Why should it matter how she dressed? Who cared if she were pretty? Part of her womanhood had died. This was a serious bereavement, and Alan needed to give more and receive more, as they rediscovered each other, alone.

Chris realises that an acceptance of what has happened is the major answer. There is no going 'back to normal', because what she now has will be 'normal' from now on. She also sees the need to regain her self-worth, and that she can still be of use; there is a lot of life left, which will be used in a different way. Like all the other parents in this chapter, she must trust both her children to God's protection, as she believes the words of Jesus that 'no-one can snatch them out of my Father's hand' (John 10:28).

The other particularly hard situation is where a previous bereavement, through death, has already happened in a family, and a member then leaves. Shirley, about whose husband's death I wrote in Chapter 6, had to let Mike go to university five years later. As a family they had been through so much, and she describes Mike's going as another bereavement. He was the first to go, and this closely-knit family found his going quite traumatic. It all brought back her husband's illness and death, because it was 'goodbye' to another family member. Of course he would come back, but it would never be the same again. With no partner for herself, Shirley was bereaved again as each child left. Finally, the house was absolutely empty. How did she survive? By learning to have a life of her own, with a job, a part to play in her church and a healthy interest in all her children, especially when one of the children kindly produced a grandchild or two, who live nearby and are glad to have Nanna around!

All these parents have proved the rightness of Alfred Torrie's words: 'It needs courage to let our children go, but we are trustees and stewards, and have to hand them back to life – to God. As the old saying puts it: "What I gave I have." We have to love them and lose them.' It is at such times I am glad to have God's promise in Hebrews 13:5: 'God has said, "Never will I leave you; never will I forsake you."' This is for us parents, and for our children too.

The last word here should be with my son Matthew, who caused this chapter to be written. I asked him how he felt on leaving home. In some ways it was a bereavement for him too, having to leave and suddenly grow up. There was so much to do for himself and, in a college where he knew absolutely no one, he was lonely and scared. It dawned on him that this was a for-ever step, and the pressure was there to return home. But he also knew how hard it had been to get to that college, and deep down he firmly believed God wanted him there. That belief strengthened his determination not to leave. Things improved when he first got reprimanded for something or other, and people started to like him for being 'real'! Friendships were formed, and he was able to be himself again. What a relief for Matthew when he found his family had not changed, and the welcome home during holidays was so special. He was the one who was changing, and growing up was OK after all. There are still big hurdles to cross, but he is proving that God does not only live in the family home, but is in his own life with him too.

Matthew's leaving was the catalyst for this whole book. I was at a conference, three weeks after he first went, and was asked to speak briefly of my recent life. Almost without thinking, I stood up and said, 'This month, I have been bereaved.' From that simple statement has come this entire book, as I have realised in how many different ways people are hurt by bereavement. Thank you, Matthew.

10

A Lost Family

Family life can be great and, as the last chapter showed, no one wants it to end. Increasingly, however, family life is little short of a tragedy for some, and we need to look at two sorts of bereavements caused by people's inability to relate to each other.

For three-and-a-half years I worked with a local authority, with responsibility for taking to court children who needed to come into the care of the authority because all was not well at home. I became aware of the traumas faced by parents and children at the break-up of family life. Now working as an evangelist, rather than a solicitor, I am still in contact with those who face this sort of bereavement – for that is what it is. In the next chapter we will look at the agonies of divorce, but here we will feel the pain of children whose lives are affected by a family which has gone wrong.

So often in a divorce, the children suffer most. Chapter 11 will show the pain of partners, but Yvonne's story encapsulates the loss for a child. Yvonne hardly knew her father, whose life was largely spent away at sea. At seven, her parents separated, and within three years her mother moved from one end of the country to the other, taking Yvonne and her younger sister with her. At the time, Yvonne apparently was able to cope, especially as she had not enjoyed a great relationship with her dad. Only as time went on did she realise her loss. Mum had to work long hours to support the girls, and Yvonne had to take responsibility for her younger sister.

Rebellion and resentment reared their ugly heads. On reflection, Yvonne now sees that her mum was doing all she could, but in her teens she felt nothing but anger and regret at her mother working so much, even to the extent of being at work on Christmas Day, with Yvonne being left to baby-sit or drift round to Gran's. She missed her dad, especially when she saw her friends with two parents, laughing with their fathers. Hurt as a teenager, angry with her mother, lonely without her father, Yvonne found her problems spilled into her own marriage. She set too high an ideal for her new family, where everything had to be perfect, not realising she was carrying ridiculous ideas of how things ought to be. To begin with she did not want children, fearing she would not be able to give them the security she herself had missed.

I realise I am in danger of appearing to say, 'Become a Christian and all will be well,' as if God waves a magic wand like a fairy godmother. Many people who become Christians find life gets more demanding, rather than less, but Yvonne found that Jesus Christ did change things for the better. Three or four years ago she became a Christian and allowed Jesus to soften her life. She found that God was her Father, and that he would not leave her, or let her down. Knowing his forgiveness, she has been able to forgive both her parents, and to see how much her mother has cared. Above all, God has healed her grieving for a lost father, and all he could have done for her. She still misses him, and wonders how to trace him, if only to send him a photo of her family. As a girl who missed out on love, Yvonne now has the love of a husband and children, to which has been added the overwhelming love of God. Psalm 10:14 says of God, 'You are the helper of the fatherless.' Yvonne has proved it in her life.

It's hard for boys too. Like Yvonne, Des had a father walk out when he was young. Des is somewhat older than Yvonne, and his father's problem was the Second World War. Rescued from the beaches of Dunkirk, he was then taken prisoner in Sicily. Later released, he was again taken prisoner in Belgium, and peacetime did not find him ready to settle down as a father. Spending most of his time in the pub, he was rarely with Des, who saw his dad hit his mother in frequent drunken brawls, ending only when his mother locked herself in the bedroom. One day Des saw him ironing his trousers and shining his brown shoes till they glistened: he was going back to the Army. 'Don't go, Dad. I love you,' were the last words of this nine-year-old to the dad he did not see again for thirty years.

What a bereavement! Des cried terribly for a long time, yearning for a dad who could do what all his mates' dads did. Slowly his grief turned to hatred for what his father had done to the family. He sided with his mum, who sacrificed everything, including her health. He felt stigmatised as the son of a broken marriage, a feeling exacerbated by being the recipient of free meals at school and hand-outs of free presents at Christmas. He recalls the pain on opening a second-hand chess set with a piece missing. He worked part time as a butcher's boy, earning six shillings a week, only to find his mother had two shillings docked by the National Assistance Board. How he hated his father!

Thirty years later, his younger brother wanted to see Dad, and traced him to a city in the North of England. A letter arrived, saying that Dad wanted to be in touch, as he was dying. The three brothers travelled North, and

Des found he was almost too scared to speak to his father. Together they went to the house and an old man answered the door. 'Tommy? We're your three boys.' 'I'm pleased to meet you,' he replied, and shook hands with the youngest son whom he had never seen.

In a wonderful way, a healing began. Des often went to visit after that, while his dad was dying of cancer of the throat. After all those years, he could not relate to him as his father, but he grew fond of him as a man, and with the way he dealt with his illness. He was able to understand a little of the pressures of war, and tried to understand his father's inability to cope with civilian and family life. It has been hard for Des to find anything positive in all this, but he is able to draw on his experience to empathise with others. God has been around for Des, as for Yvonne, and meeting his father helped to heal his childhood. Life had been darkness and desolation, but now he does not feel rejected.

For me, the most positive thing to emerge from all this has been the way Des and his wife Valerie have turned this dreadful negative into a glorious positive. The Bible says, 'Religion that God our Father accepts as pure and faultless is this: to look after orphans and widows in their distress and to keep oneself from being polluted by the world' (James 1:27). Instead of allowing his life to remain embittered, Des has given his suffering over to God to enable good to come out of it. Des and Valerie now foster children whose own families cannot, or will not, cope with them, and so provide the sort of home Des wishes he could have had. That means entering into the anguish those children feel and exhibit. However awful the situation has been, a child feels bereaved of his or her familiar surroundings, and the love – however small – of family and friends. Des remembers three children, totally abandoned by their parents, found living on their own in terrible squalor. The policemen who found them cooked them bacon and eggs and removed them to a foster home. But those children still grieved for the squalor and the parents who had abandoned them. It was 'home', and they had known love. Confused, frightened and crying, they beat the police with their fists as they were removed from their appalling conditions.

As a child is fostered or adopted, there will probably be a 'honeymoon' period, when all is quiet. Then will come an explosion of naughtiness, as the child goes through a period of bereavement. Part of the reason this happens is because they now feel secure enough to do it; safe enough to exhibit anger, even to the extent of wrecking the place. The older a child is, the worse the grieving. But, as Des and Valerie prove, if children are cared for and loved, given food, warmth and a cosy bed, they can quickly adapt. In some cases this adaptation is simply because a child has become 'street-wise' after several moves from one foster home to another.

Inevitably, a fostered child brings all his emotional baggage with him. Des and Valerie remember one five-year-old lad who would ask several times each hour, 'You all right, Auntie Val?' His mother was mentally ill, and he had had to look after all her needs, constantly checking her welfare.

Valerie watches for the tell-tale signs of the bereavement of a family in her foster children. One will carry books all round the house, another will soil her clothes and many will regress when they come into new surroundings. One boy cried all day, and would only stop when Valerie – and only Valerie – picked him up. Small children would simply be bewildered, needing a mother figure. Valerie feels that the main way to help a child in this type of bereavement situation is to give that child time – even more than love. They will not get over their lifetime of hurts in an afternoon.

Simon is one of Des and Valerie's most special people, because they have now adopted him. Simon has been hard work, not least because he was born suffering with his mother's drug addiction. His bereavement at losing his mother, who has since died, is helped by Des and Valerie being honest with him. He knows they are not his natural parents, but that he is very special, as they have chosen voluntarily to have him as their son. His great problem is one of confusion: he thinks all children have an 'old mummy'! Knowing something of Simon's background, they are able to understand his bad temper and help him control it. It is lovely to see how special his love is for Des.

In this family, Valerie and Des are doing two vital things. They are allowing Des' bereavement of his family to mould their getting it right, so a most positive result emerges from a tragic past. And they are bringing God's love to their children – natural, adopted and fostered. God loves these hurt and lost children, and Des and Valerie prove this to them. 'Can a mother forget the baby at her breast and have no compassion on the child she has borne? Though she may forget, I will not forget you! See, I have engraved you on the palms of my hands' (Isaiah 49:15–16). This promise of God is not just for his people thousands of years ago, but for all of us today, and not least those children who feel rejected in any way. And it is people like Valerie and Des who prove it to them, not just in kindly words, but by making it happen.

If, thus far, I have given the impression that I think this sort of bereavement is always easy to work through, I am about to put the record straight with the cautionary tale of John and Julie, two of the loveliest people I know. Their lives have been made all but impossible by one of their two adopted sons. With two older sons of their own, they were willing to foster a couple of 'problem' children, and so two brothers – Lee aged two and Steven aged four – arrived, badly abused and hospitalised by a desperate mother. The good news is that Lee, a quadriplegic with cerebral palsy, has totally bonded with them. He tells Julie, 'You're my mummy. I just grew in another lady's tummy.' He remembers nothing of life before fostering, and is delightfully happy, despite all his problems. Both boys have now been adopted.

But Steven is a different story. Terribly abused physically and mentally by four, he has never recovered. He showed his anger at once, by crying, stamping, slamming doors and deliberately soiling his bed. Eight years on, he is still suffering all the wrong reactions to his bereavement of being separated from his natural mother and father. His social workers never told him anything, and now Julie dreads the day he discovers the truth. Happily, social work practice is changing, and children as young as three now receive counselling as to why they have been taken into care. It is doubtful whether Steven will be able to believe the truth, and the fear of his reaction prevents any moves towards his being told. He is unable to cope with discipline, and life at home with him is all but impossible. He seems totally confused, sometimes acting very childishly, and, at other times, like a very old man.

The quality of life in the home is often at zero, and John and Julie themselves feel bereaved of the adopted child they had hoped for and of what might have been. No one seems to have an answer, and few seem to understand. They cannot imagine life without him, but can hardly face life with him. Steven seems unable to get through any of the stages of bereavement, leaving them grieving too. They are grateful for, and helped by, the prayers of friends, and are trusting God to get them through. At least Steven is now at an age when they can point out the consequences of his delinquency. Also, John and Julie are receiving counselling, which helps a lot. But, as Julie told me, she still misses *her* father, who died over thirty years ago, so how do Lee and Steven feel?

As with some of the other bereavements in this book, this one is awaiting a solution. In talking with a former colleague, we agreed this is inevitable. Pam was a leading social worker with a local authority when I was that authority's Social Services' solicitor, and she recalled cases where children's problems never fully went away. A man in his fifties continues to feel guilty for being dumped into care by his parents, as if it were his fault, despite it not being anything to do with him. Pam says he will never overcome it, but it does make him a good father. Many a child will feel guilt like this, which can be combatted later by telling that child the real truth about what went wrong. Alas, that leads to another bereavement, when the child realises his parents were not like other parents, and a new guilt sets in.

Some children will accept their lot, especially if the parent exhibits obvious problems, such as mental illness or drunkenness. Yet I recall a teenager in care who hanged himself when his parents' marriage broke up, despite his home being extremely well off and he being in no way to blame. Pam feels that as much honesty as possible is the best policy, despite the hurts that will bring. If the blame is with the child, he or she needs to work through their wrong. Usually it is not their fault that they have lost their family, and they need to be helped to be cleared of the guilt they feel. But how hard it is to live with the knowledge that you have two very problematic people at the back of you!

Someone who has lost their family in this way needs a great deal of careful handling. Much of the help needed is practical, caring and long term. A child who left or who was left by the family when very young, or much older, may cope better than one aged between two and ten. In every case, we must handle with care. For any who have suffered in this way, it is helpful if they can be encouraged to look forward, not back. One of the greatest tragedies in the Bible is when Jesus said to the city of Jerusalem, 'How often I have longed to gather your children together, as a hen gathers her chicks under her wings, but you were not willing' (Matthew 23:37). Whoever else is shut out it is important for the individual not to close God out. He wants to gather us in, as the most loving parent of all, to the warmth and love of his everlasting family.

11

Death of a Marriage

Children do get hurt when relationships fail. But so do the principal participants, and the bereavement caused by a divorce is real, deep and lasting. In the last chapter we saw something of the child's hurt. Now here is the second loss: that of the partners themselves. When I was at university obtaining a law degree in the early sixties, the divorce rate in England and Wales was one divorce for every six marriages. We, as emerging lawyers, were horrified lest this rate should sink to the then American level of one in four. Now, these few years later, more than one marriage in three ends in divorce and, if present trends continue, the rate will be one divorce for every marriage by the year 2010.

I am one of the lucky ones, with a very happy marriage. Having worked as a solicitor in private practice for a number of years, I have had close contact with very many marriage breakdowns, and have seen the depth of bereavement these have caused. I have no intention of sitting in judgement, but I do want to consider the problem and try to point a way through the hurts and loss, so hopelessness does not set in. It is not for me to condemn – this is a book which is meant to suggest answers. The wife, the husband and the wider family all feel a divorce keenly, and have to cope differently.

How do people get through? Let's take ladies first.

'Irene' and 'William' married young and William was unwilling, or unable, to give up his outside interests. By the time their first son was born two years later, the relationship had deteriorated to a dangerous point and Irene frequently found herself wandering the streets in despair. She tried and tried to make the marriage work, but even a change of house did not rekindle the fires. She thought about a girl she knew who had married when six months pregnant. It seemed so unfair that this girl should be so happy, while Irene herself, having tried to be so good, was now facing a disaster. In the wings hovered 'Victor' and she sought solace in his arms. William sued for divorce, and Irene felt total guilt, as if her very life had come to an end. Victor bought out William's share of the matrimonial home, but Irene found it impossible to live with Victor simply in place of William, and her guilt and churning inside drove Victor away. Overpowered by emotion, Irene went with her two children back to Mum and Dad.

'Where have you ever been happy?' she asked herself. To her surprise, she replied, 'Church.' So she went. There she heard of God's love, and how she could hand her life over to the Jesus from whom she had turned away. She discovered what it meant to be 'born again' and to have a new beginning with God. But her problems were still there, and Irene knew that the mess she was in was one she deserved. As she started to pick up her life, William returned to the scene, joining her at church. It was time for another try, and they remarried. Within three months, things fell apart again, and William left. Irene faced more tears, but at least she now had help and counselling from her minister and others at the church. Being a Christian, she felt even more guilty, as if the whole church was watching her: the first time she had committed adultery, the second time she had again rejected William, closing the door with, 'Enough's enough.' No one ever told her she had done wrong, but she felt that was what they were saying.

In an attitude of resignation, Irene felt she would never be loved, or married. She threw herself into looking after her children, running the house and working. This time it was William who had an affair, and they were divorced again. In many ways this brought Irene relief. The first time had been the deep bereavement, but there comes a time when one has no more strength or ability to grieve. Back from the wings came Victor, and she finally married him. Now the two of them are letting Jesus hold them together, as they accept his forgiveness. Her marriages to William seem like an awful dream, and enable her to draw alongside many with marriage and divorce problems, to show that they can get through. People ask Irene how, as a Christian, she can cope with being remarried. She admits that there is nothing in the Bible which gives her an answer, which makes her sad. 'How do I stand?' she asks. 'In the grace of God.' It's a great answer – and the only one there is. When we throw ourselves on the love we do not deserve, God is able to forgive us and make us new.

But what a mess we can find ourselves in! 'Naomi' would agree with that: her big mistake was to marry 'Frank' on the rebound. Just divorced, she met Frank at work, a tall, dark, younger man who made a bee-line for this very beautiful lady. Naomi describes the whole affair as having a 'Mills & Boon' quality – the urgent 'I love you' phone calls, the weekly flowers, the sudden Christmas Eve wedding – so romantic. From there it was downhill all the way. Neither could cope with their first child's birth, and Frank moved out. Naomi was resentful and lonely, and became clinically depressed. During periods of attempted reconciliation there were dreadful fights and violent rows. Craziest of all, they decided another baby would give a new beginning. Not a good idea! Like Irene, in her despair Naomi turned to God, and was helped to become a Christian by a lady at church.

It was too late to save the marriage, and Frank told her to get out and never come back. Naomi was distraught, with a feeling of enormous guilt, as if she should have known this would happen, and that Frank would not be able to cope. She felt to blame, as if she should have spotted some clue that Frank would do this, and she felt she had let the children down. Why had she got married in the first place, after a previous failed marriage? 'I don't have the sense I was born with!' she told me.

Has she been able to recover? Yes, she has. Naomi received lots of counselling from those trained in sorting out this type of bereavement, and she has felt God's healing too. One special thing was to visit Frank a final time, when she was able to see there was no hope for them. The morning after their meeting, she awoke with Charles Wesley's words in her thoughts: 'My chains fell off, my heart was free.'

When I talked with Naomi, she told me a remarkable thing. She had heard once of how a shepherd would break the leg of a straying lamb, and then hold that lamb tight so it grew to love the shepherd in his safe keeping. 'God broke both my arms and legs so I could love him!' is how she describes his rescue of her. Now, knowing God is there and will never leave her, she has lost her regrets and inadequacy.

Although Naomi has come through, she would agree that the experience has been terrible, as it is for the vast majority of those who experience marriage failure. Hilary goes so far as to call it the worst experience of her life. Married to Brian, and with two children, their marriage ended after he had admitted to two other relationships. Both Christians, Hilary could not understand how God would let this happen and hoped that, by seeking help, everything would be fine. Willing to forgive Brian, she realised he only wanted to be out of the marriage. 'I had this incredible sense of loss,' Hilary told me. 'I had lost my husband, the children's father, my marriage, my friend, companion and provider, and my self-respect. It was just like a death, but at least when a loved one has died you have happy memories, and the knowledge that they loved you.' Rejected and betrayed, she still has to see Brian twice a week as he calls for the children, and he spends much of his time with his new lady-friend near Hilary's home.

Hilary admits to crying, screaming, shouting and desperately asking God why he let all this happen. Even now, some years after the divorce, there are days when she feels low. How has she come through? First, by trusting God to have a plan for her life. Then by realising he has not abandoned her. The devil does not have the last word, nor must she place too much reliance on anyone or anything else other than God alone. Her children, family and friends have encouraged her, and her deep feelings for Brian have gone. Now she is seeking the strength from God to forgive him: the hardest step of all.

Like Hilary, 'Gill' looks back on her broken marriage as a worse bereavement than that caused by death, because she will never know if her husband 'Eddy' was really happy. She thought all was well, till one evening after an argument Eddy announced he was sleeping on the sofa. When Gill went to apologise, he told her things had been building up for a long time, and asked her to leave as soon as she could. With no previous inkling that anything was wrong, she was profoundly shocked, even thinking Eddy was having a breakdown. No one else was

involved on either side, and Gill stayed for some time trying to recover the marriage.

In her worry she could not sleep. She walked the
streets and contemplated suicide. In desperation, she
even wondered about having at least one of their three
children adopted. In the end Eddy went to live with his
father, and Gill had no alternative but to move. When
they next met, she still tried to persuade him they could
change, and try again. But Eddy's feelings were strong,
and it was all over. He never told Gill why he ended the
marriage, and to this day she does not know. She has
cried a lot, and has unashamedly drawn on a wide circle
of friends for support and prayer, writing hundreds of
letters to them. Her three children gave her a purpose in
life, but she missed having her husband's arms around
her, and their sexual relationship. As a Christian, she was
very unsure about marrying again, but she realised that if
God could forgive a convicted murderer then he could
forgive a failed marriage. She had tried so hard, and now
finds fulfilment in helping others who feel they have no
future after a divorce. Now remarried, Gill has not let her
bad experiences ruin her for ever.

So much for the ladies! In divorce, men often get a
very bad press, and I'm not going to defend unacceptable
behaviour, but men do feel bereaved by marriage failure
too. A recent newspaper article related how one man had
come home to find a note saying his wife had left, and
how he felt passion, anger, resentment, sorrow and guilt.
Men do feel those things, though they often find it hard
either to admit it or to express those feelings. A man's
pride especially gets hurt, and that was Mike's major
feeling of bereavement.

Mike was married to Beverley, but his job as a musician
meant he was often away from home, and his 5am home-
comings left him lying on the settee each day, useless to

wife and children alike. Anyone can be wise after the event, and Mike now sees that things would have been better if he had found himself a 'proper job' as he calls it, and tried to be a better husband and father. His two children rarely saw him, and Beverley became involved with another man, later going to live with him.

What is bereavement in a broken marriage? Mike's is a classic situation in many ways. 'It is the loss of a love affair,' he says. Mike and Beverley went out for seven years before getting married when he was twenty-two, and he lost all that love and youthful passion when the marriage ended. His pride was hurt when he discovered his wife wanted someone other than him, and the other women he got involved with did not bring him the happiness he had known. He lost his trust: he would be playing his music in a bar half a mile from his home, and would go home during the interval to spy through the window to see if anyone was there. Once, he went in through the front door as a man ran out of the back. It would be funny if it were not so tragic.

Mike's bereavement happened during the marriage, as it slowly disintegrated. It continued during the divorce itself, as he found the court case a humiliating experience. The final blow came from his younger son, who had been living with him after the divorce (the older boy living with Beverley). On a visit to the zoo one day, his son said, 'Daddy, I don't like you any more. I want to go to Mummy.'

'If you want to,' Mike replied. 'I'll take you.' But it broke his heart. Mike's recovery has not been easy, but he has now married again, and his younger son moved back with him some years later. Much later, Mike also became a Christian, and he has discovered God's forgiveness. But there has been no easy way out. Anyone looking at his marriage would have said he was to blame for its failure, but none the less his bereavement was real and painful, and condemnation must be tempered by compassion.

In a divorce, both partners lose a great deal, but sometimes one partner will feel they have lost almost everything. In the last chapter we met Des and Valerie. Some years before Valerie appeared on the scene, Des was married to Ann. After a stormy marriage, Ann left, and Des had nothing: Ann not only took the two children, she took all their possessions too. Des was left with the cutlery! He felt empty: his wife was with another man, and all they had made together had vanished in a moment. He even received letters from the children, apparently dictated by Ann – or so he believed – saying they did not want to see him. He drowned his sorrow in beer and wallowed in self-pity.

He came through this grieving because people helped him. At work, a colleague, who was a Christian, lost his baby daughter through a cot death. Des went to the funeral, and saw that as this massive, gentle man carried the coffin of his child, his Christian faith stood firm. Des realised that he had two living children, but his attitude had been one of giving in and misery. When he got drunk, another Christian workmate would see him home and be a good friend to him. These people had a secret to living, a relationship with God and victory in tragedy. As these men showed Jesus to Des, and shared his love, Des slowly let God change his life. Chapter 10 shows how much better things are now.

What a sad chapter this is! So much of the problem lies in the lack of any neat conclusion and the deep sense of guilt and condemnation felt by one or both partners. Whereas being a Christian helps most bereavements, it is often a serious disadvantage to be a Christian when a marriage fails, as the story of 'Oliver' and 'Zara' showed me. Perhaps they should never have got married: Oliver

was 'on the rebound', and both were infatuated with
each other, rather than in love. Both had doubts, but fear
of adverse comments took them through the wedding.
The marriage never worked, but being central figures in
a Christian community meant appearances had to be
kept up.

Two children were born, but often the home resem-
bled World War Three. Oliver and Zara had totally different interests, and they drifted apart. Both worked all
hours, and Oliver often had to act as both father and
mother. Zara's unhappiness took her into an affair, and
she left. In talking with Oliver, he spoke of how Zara was
confused and in such a mess, as she was bereaved of
being with her children. For him it meant loneliness,
without his woman. He grieved for the good times, and
for his hurting children, who would sit on the bed and
cry, 'I want my mummy back.' Oliver was broken by their
tears. He would visit places they had been to together,
and his eyes would fill with tears. The bad times would be
forgotten as he wished they could get together again, but
it was not to be.

Oliver's work involves helping people bereaved by
death, and he (like Hilary earlier) feels his divorce is
worse than a death: he has lost the person with whom he
has shared his life in the most intimate way, and yet she is
still around, and they have to keep in touch for the children. The house is still his, but the pain of her absence is
only heightened by knowing that she is somewhere else.
The scars never go: the stress and pain of living with Zara
were replaced by the grief and loss of her departure.
Insecure, fearful and anxious, Oliver was very fragile
emotionally, even after he met and subsequently married
'Ursula'.

As a Christian, Oliver found that church leaders were
unable to cope, and failed to give him any support. It was

the ordinary, quiet Christians who drew alongside with their sympathy. Time has had to be the real healer, together with a deep experience of God's forgiveness. Oliver knows he has got it wrong, and that Zara is no more to blame than he is. But he accepts God's promise: 'If we confess our sins, he is faithful and just and will forgive us our sins' (1 John 1:9). He now knows God's blessings, and is able to help others with their marriage problems. Although he enjoys a good relationship with Ursula, he is still saddened that he and Zara failed.

Now he and Ursula have to work very hard on the new relationships between her and Oliver's children, which has not proved at all easy. In this type of bereavement, the loss felt by the children must always be at the forefront of people's minds. Adding in a new partner is an additional pressure on those children, and the whole family feels the painful establishing of the new life. The parents of the divorced couple feel it too. A divorce is never done in isolation: the whole family is in it. I realised this when I met Jean, the mother of a divorcee.

Jean has three sons, but only the middle one married. His wife became the daughter Jean had never had, and their separation broke Jean's heart. Being one step removed, she had no inkling that anything was wrong, and wishes she could have talked with them before it was too late. Her son phoned every day after the separation, and Jean cried with him and for him. She missed her 'daughter', and there was no one to talk to about how she herself felt. Devastated, Jean would break down and weep as she drove her car. Although she was used to helping others through her work with the Samaritans, she felt it was worse than a death in the family: her 'daughter' was around, but out of reach. Ten years after the separation and divorce, Jean feels she will never be the same again. Her grief was private and alone, as her son and other family members carried their own hurts. Jean has tried to concentrate on not being bitter, or blaming anyone, and has tried to get over it slowly. But it has been deeply painful.

As I have tried to show, how Jean feels is how most people feel about divorce. The loose ends fray. The guilt, loneliness, loss and heartbreak are exacerbated by 'if onlys', and by the continuing life elsewhere of the other partner, to say nothing of the children. In trying to help someone in this situation, we need to be careful not to condemn.

For those in this situation, it may help if they can allow the anger to surface sometimes, and remember the negatives! I often think that the opening verses of Psalm 130 were written for people such as these: 'Out of the depths I cry to you, O Lord; O Lord, hear my voice. Let your ears be attentive to my cry for mercy. If you, O Lord, kept a record of sins, O Lord, who could stand? But with you there is forgiveness' (Psalm 130:1–4).

As Jesus said, 'Everyone who sins is a slave to sin . . . [but] if the Son sets you free, you will be free indeed' (John 8:34, 36).

12

Raped

Bereavement, as the dictionary tells us, is having someone or something precious stolen away from you. It sug-
gests a tearing, like a robbery, and nothing fits this
aggressive definition more nearly than rape. However difficult it is for those who know little or nothing about rape
to read this chapter, this book would not be complete
without it. Every person who has talked with me about
their losses and bereavements has shown great courage
in opening up their private griefs, but none more so than
those in the next few pages. As with some other chapters,
I feel I am not able to deal with this hurt adequately, and
others have written more fully and helpfully. In most
cases, I am not commending any other particular works;
but in this instance I must mention an excellent booklet
called *Rape as Bereavement* by Judy Hanson, published by
Grove Books of Bramcote, Nottinghamshire. In it, we are
shown how the rape victim needs to go through the grieving process, and how the whole subject needs to be much
more understood by the vast majority of the population
who know so little about it.

For those who have suffered this violation, or who are
trying to help and understand someone who has been,
perhaps Christine, 'Maureen' and 'Jade' will be able to
show a way through. Christine was on what was supposed

to be the holiday of a lifetime, when her lifetime fell apart. For a fortnight, she and a girlfriend had enjoyed the beaches and sights each day, and the local cafés each night. On the last evening before returning to England, they lingered at their favourite café, and it seemed quite natural to accept a lift back to their hotel offered by two of the young men who had been their waiters during their stay.

Driving along the coast, the girls reluctantly agreed to a quick walk on the beach, and Christine's friend and one of the men ran off together. In a moment, the pleasant easy-going young waiter who stayed with Christine became an aggressive man who told her, with English and foreign swear words, to get out and do as she was told. It was pitch-dark, the others had gone, there was no traffic and the only sound was the sea. She was pulled from the car, and they walked onto the beach. For twenty minutes, Christine kept him talking, till he told her what he intended. Her mind racing, knowing what would happen, she realised the situation was impossible. There was nowhere to run – especially with the sea so near – and no one to call to, as the man said that Christine's friend was suffering the same fate (which turned out to be completely untrue).

She thought the men had both planned it all, and everything in her froze. He threatened her with violence if she resisted, and in vain she clung to her dress. For another half hour she tried to stop him, but inevitably he did rape her, aggressively and deliberately. As she shut down emotionally and physically, Christine at least knew she could face death unafraid. The man reacted nonchalantly, as if little had happened, while Christine was in total shock. Back at the car she could say nothing till they reached the hotel, when she simply told her friend, 'He raped me.' The other man was shocked, and Christine

was taken to hospital, bleeding heavily. There, no sympathy was shown, and no treatment offered, till a statement
was given to the police. She had been injured and
needed further treatment in England for infection. Six
months later, the Court heard the man's case in Christine's absence, and he was found not guilty of rape.

But for Christine herself, her whole life was shattered.
She wept as she felt the man had left his dirtiness in her,
and she agonised for nearly three weeks till she could be
certain she was not pregnant. Unable to tell her family,
she made up a story about missing the plane. Her friend
did not know what to do, and felt guilty for not being
there to help. This feeling eventually caused her to end
her friendship with Christine.

Five months later Christine left her work and went
abroad, running away from the people who knew what
had happened. Even her church minister told her in so
many words that what had happened was her own fault,
and that God would have protected her if she had been
acting in the right way. It takes a long time to get over the
stupid and irresponsible comment that a Christian who
gets raped deserves it. Christine tried to forget the whole
thing, but was twice further assaulted, though not raped,
during the following year: once by a drunk who grabbed
her in the street. She came to the conclusion that no man
could be trusted.

I have told Christine's story in some detail to show how
much there was for her to get over, and how desperate a
bereavement rape is. Has Christine recovered, and, if so,
how? When she returned to England, she went to college,
and was helped by meeting men who knew nothing of
her past, and who did not threaten her. But for three
years she was unable to go out with anyone, nor could she
face being alone with any man – even to the extent of
being unwilling to ride in a lift with a lone male. Scared

of men as a group, she could not even accept a hug. Before the rape she had had boyfriends. Now relationships were totally different. Christine felt violated in every way: physically, mentally, emotionally and spiritually. Only after about five years did things start to change.

A Christian when the incident happened, Christine came to the realisation that, in some way, God himself had been raped with her. He had not left her, and he wanted to heal her. A few close friends made her feel valuable, but the church in general seemed to be poor in dealing with the issues of sex. A major problem was that she had lost her right to choose regarding her use of sex, and she realised that any person with whom she entered a relationship would have to come to terms with that too. Christine now accepts that this is something which, like any great and sudden bereavement, will affect her throughout her life. It is part of her, and she cannot change what has happened. But this is also very positive, because this acceptance means she is able to live with the different person she has become. Given the fact that it happened, and that rotten things happen to many people, she is not going to let it destroy her.

In talking with Christine, I found her to be an extremely positive, happy and fulfilled lady. A major reason for this was her ability to place the guilt where it really lay. She was not the one to blame, so her feelings of guilt have stopped spiralling. For her own sake she has needed to forgive the man, seeing him as part of the sad selfishness of this world. Realistically, Christine does not foresee absolute, complete healing on earth, though part of her hopes that a final healing of her bereavement might come in a good sexual relationship with a future husband, and she can now view that possibility without fear. As she has given this whole grief over to God, Christine has found what he said in Exodus 15:26 is true: 'I am the Lord, who heals you.'

That is the ultimate way through, and 'Maureen' had to discover that too. Her rape was by a complete stranger, and is a worrying indictment on our way of life in Britain. Cycling home from a church function one evening, her bike broke down. A man she had passed came up from behind and put his hand over her mouth, threatening to knife her. In panic, she tried to cry out, but the houses on her side of the road were set back, and there was a park on the other side. Such is the state of our society that the man was able to hold Maureen in his grip as they waited for several cars to pass before they went over the road, to the dark and seclusion of the park.

Here was the place of no hope. She was told to let go of her bike and take off her clothes, with more threats from the knife. Would she die? Would she see her family again? With these thoughts, Maureen tried to reason with the man, who told her to shut up. Almost naked, she had to lie in the mud while the man struggled with his drunkenness to fulfil himself. He asked her if she was a virgin, and she said that she was, and that she was a Christian too. Whereupon he struck her face, and she prayed. At no time did she feel God deserted her, and in the end the man was disturbed by a passer-by. He tied her up, and made her promise not to tell. Then he rode off on her broken bike. She was able to free herself, put on a few clothes and get to a friend's house. The police were splendid, helping her put together an Identikit picture which led to the man's arrest nine days later.

So began those indications of bereavement which such a violent rape brings. Maureen was afraid, panicking as she lay in bed, thinking a stopping car was the man returning to punish her for telling. She was angry that someone would do this, not just to her, but as one human

being to another. However, she did feel the man had
damaged his own life more than hers, so her anger did
not go to the extent of a neighbour's, who said that all
rapists should be castrated. In some ways she felt sorry for
him. Her main problem was one of vulnerability, as she
became ultra-nervous about going out at night, or of
being alone, and only time has resolved this. It was hard
to talk about what had happened, as she would burst
into tears. Anyway, it was not wise to tell everyone: most
people do not know how to react and many cannot cope.
Carrying on as normal proved a good policy. Having one
or two close friends on whom she could off-load her
deepest thoughts and scream at was good too.

Waiting for the man's trial was especially stressful, and
his plea of guilty was a huge relief. He got six-and-a-half
years. But the vulnerability was not all negative and
Maureen is now able to empathise with others who feel
threatened by life and its problems. And, of course, she
was hurt, and she felt as if someone had put a knife down
her throat to her very middle, and turned it. Now, some
years later, the emotional scar is still there, and times like
the anniversary of the rape prove difficult.

As with Christine, I have been most impressed with
Maureen's reaction to God in all this. Never feeling abandoned by him, she was aware of many people's prayers
for her. Others may ask where God had been, and how
she could believe in a loving God when this awful thing
had happened, but she rightly says that being a Christian
gives her no special immunity to the bad things that happen. God comes, not to remove all suffering, but to be in
it with us; not to stop all evil, but to show that the pit is
not bottomless. Maureen was also able to accept that her
healing would take time. She realised that when someone
dies, those bereaved are not expected to get over their
loss quickly, and the pain will still be there, even though

they appear to be living normal lives. The hurt will go gradually, but they will never forget. So it was with Maureen, and she has slowly but surely come through her grief, although from time to time she still needs to accept a re-emergence of the hurt, and more healing.

Most touchingly, she has understood in a very deep and personal way what Christ must have suffered on the cross: naked, humiliated, physically assaulted and utterly powerless. Though the rape was horrendous, she feels privileged, in a strange sort of way. And she also realises many people will find that a very odd reaction! Because of that cross, Maureen is able to be 'perfect in Christ' (Colossians 1:28), and her rape is not a devastating end. She has been able to get married too, to a man who proves to her that there is some good in some of us.

'Jade' has found that too, in her marriage to 'Rob'; that there is a love which can be known between a man and a woman, and a happy sexual relationship. They now have a small son. If ever anyone needed to find this it was Jade, whose story in some ways is the most tragic of all. As far back as she can remember, she was sexually abused by her grandfather. Certainly by the age of eight she was having to perform all sorts of disgusting sexual acts with him – some of them so terrible she has never been able to verbalise them. She is almost certain her mother had suffered similarly, and all but sure she knew what was happening. Even her grandmother was aware: Jade recalls an occasion when her gran stood in the doorway watching, and then turned away.

What a way to grow up, unable to resist, and growing into a 'yes' person. Her only hope was to feign sleep, or to say she was having a period. Then at the age of seventeen Jade finally said 'no'. Soon afterwards, her grandfather died. What a bereavement, or rather a set of bereavements, she faced. She was bereaved of her virginity, and used to think she would never be able to walk up the aisle in white when she got married. She was bereaved of a family, as she could not talk to anyone, knowing the family would be destroyed if she said anything. To go to her grandfather's funeral was the last thing she wanted to do. There was no one to whom she could turn.

A whole childhood was taken from her; snatched away by a man who could have made it beautiful. Before she was able to experience the joys of innocence and halcyon, carefree days, she was plunged into an adult world of shame, hurts and secrecy. She has become aware of this particularly as she now has a child of her own. As he grows, her husband reminisces about his happy upbringing, with long, sunny, summer days enjoyed with friends. He realises there must have been other days, but they have faded from memory. By contrast, Jade cannot remember one happy day from her childhood. She tries really hard to recall birthdays, Christmas and holidays, but the whole past is dark with doom and gloom. Like Rob, she knows there must have been another side, but for her the pain covers everything like a blanket.

How does one ever emerge from such a life of continual rape and abuse? In talking with Jade, three strands emerge. At Number One, she would put her husband's love and help. He is helping her to become stronger, and to discover the person she is meant to be. As they grow in their love, so the non-love of her grandfather fades. Rob accepts her as she is, and is seeing her through.

Secondly, Jade has accepted good, professional counselling. Writing her story down for counsellors has been therapeutic, and she is still aware of her vulnerability. Some of the writing and counselling has been exhausting, but it has also proved a release. There has not been a specific moment when all has suddenly changed, but there have been a number of times when she has moved forward significantly.

There have also been times of regression. Not long ago, Jade had her handbag stolen at church, and she felt that some man (it did not cross her mind that it might be a woman!) must know everything about her: where she lived, where she worked, had all her keys, and so on. She felt again that a man had invaded her. After coping for a week, she had to go to the church when the building was dark, and she felt the man was waiting to 'get' her. From deep down inside she wept, and found further healing through the release of her tears.

And Jade is so glad that her third help has come from God's love, and from the Bible. Like many who are bereaved, Jade has found great encouragement from God's promise in Isaiah 43:18–19: 'Forget the former things; do not dwell on the past. See, I am doing a new thing! Now it springs up; do you not perceive it? I am making a way in the desert and streams in the wasteland.' As she still fights negative feelings, and still has to relate to her mother and grandmother, she is having to trust God for his help as she tries to forgive them, even if she will never be able to talk with them about all that happened. There has been no magic wand cure, but God is there with her. With Rob, Jade is learning God's way forward, and Jesus makes her feel loved and special.

That must be the way of it. After all, why should the rapist win? The cross may be seen as a sort of 'raping' of God – but resurrection was around the corner. For the victim of rape, resurrection may come slowly. Christine, Maureen and Jade can testify that there is a way through.

13

A New Home

American evangelist Billy Graham told of how he was in the lift of a London hotel when the lift operator said to him, 'We've got one of your fellow-countrymen staying here.'

'Oh,' said Billy. 'Who's that?'

'Billy Graham.'

'That's me!' he grinned, at which the man looked him up and down and, after a pause, merely commented, 'Boy, what an anti-climax!'

After the emotions of the last chapter, this one may feel something of a let-down, but we might identify with it none the less, as we remember the traumas of moving, and the pain it brought, as well as the pleasure. When my wife and I moved to the Midlands from our more native North of England, we left a loving, caring, friendly neighbourhood and church to come to a city where we knew no one, and from where it was too far to keep running 'home'. It was much harder to make this move than we thought, and a great deal of adjustment had to take place.

The excitement of new horizons is tempered by the bereavement of what is left behind, and some people are for ever looking over their shoulder at what was, which mars the what could be. How do people win through such difficulties?

I know it seems obvious, but our bereavement will depend on who or what we leave, and how attached we were to them. For my wife, her hardest move was when she married me! Ruth was one of those increasingly rare people who get married from the house in which they were born, and we started our life together over 300 miles south west of there. Everything was new, and she was bereaved of so much. It was goodbye to childhood, and the very close family where that had been shared. It is only when you leave home that you realise how much you have taken for granted.

Becoming a grown-up can be traumatic, especially if it happens suddenly, as it did for Ruth. All those adult responsibilities crowd in – the cooking, the shopping, the washing – all made doubly hard when there is no one to turn to other than a new husband who is also learning with you. Old friends are left behind, and a new neighbourhood means you do not know where to shop, or how to find the best bargains. But it is a great adventure, if you make it so. And we did. We were welcomed by a most friendly church, and discovered together the strength God brings to a new relationship. Several moves later, and a marriage of over twenty years, it would be fair to say that Ruth survived. Not that she does not have the odd moment of nostalgia when Northumberland is featured on the television. . . .

Sometimes there has to be a deep trust in God that he knows what he is doing. Our move to the Midlands was like that. Having gone back North, Ruth and I had that restlessness of spirit which suggested another job move. I applied all round our own area, but nothing came of interviews. The Midlands was outside our experience, as was the job I surprisingly got. Ruth and I felt it was so right to move, though we often asked why. We felt in step with God, and believed that great Bible promise of his:

'Whether you turn to the right or to the left, your ears will hear a voice behind you, saying, "This is the way; walk in it"' (Isaiah 30:21). When, over three years later, I became an evangelist who travelled all over Britain, it became so obvious that the only place we could live was where we were, in the very centre of England, and we recognised God's brilliant planning. But at the time of the move, we both felt badly bereaved at leaving a great church, a delightful neighbourhood and an accent we understood!

At least we did not have unrealistic expectations, which our friend Julie seemed to have when she made her move. Like Ruth, she had lived in the same place all her life and now, married with a child, she and her husband yearned for the countryside. One day she drove to the hills just to see green fields, and her husband hunted for a new job. Perhaps they should have thought more carefully before he accepted one in the far South West, such a very long way from their Midlands roots, but move they did.

Julie had assumed it would be easy to start again, to make friends, and she was surprised how difficult it turned out. In her new town, mothers did not meet at the school gate, and church circles were difficult to break into, partly because her husband did not share her interests there, and she was neither family nor single. Where were all her many friends, especially those who had been around for years and years? The new neighbourhood was all she had hoped for, and the coastline and fresh air were extra bonuses. But in several years she has not fully got over the loneliness, and friendships are not as deep. She can only ask God to be nearer to her, and to help her build a new life. The grass is not greener, after all.

For Ann and Francis, it could have been the same, but they have seen it through more successfully. Their move took them from one side of the country to the other as

Francis pursued a better job, and they agreed it was right to go. Knowing no one, the first couple of days left them feeling very lost. The chaos of getting two children to a new school took her time at first, but then Francis went off to work and Ann was alone, with no phone and a feeling of isolation. There was a desperate desire to 'go back home', and she hated having to make an effort to get to know new people, and the need to familiarise herself with a strange environment.

Ann made a decision which was at the same time brave and eminently sensible: this new place was to be 'home'. There was no point in trying to run away by going back across the country most weekends, using the children as an excuse to see their grandparents. Escapism would prove nothing; getting stuck in was the way to survive, and to win. With this resolve, Ann found a response in the district, as neighbours welcomed her friendliness and they had coffee together. The children were a 'plus' in this too, as she became familiar with the clinic, the nursery, the school and the shops, and got to know those who worked there. A welcoming church was glad to see a new, positive family: as they gave themselves, so they received. Now, several years later, Ann says that if Francis died, she would stay in her home, because that is what it is – home.

I believe this splendidly positive approach is the best answer to the potential bereavement of moving. I heard a lovely story from India, where an old man was sitting outside a town, when a family came by with all their possessions on a cart. 'We're moving here,' said the father to the old man. 'What are the people like?'

'What were they like in the town you've left?' the old man asked back.

'Oh, they were very friendly. We loved them.'

'I'm happy to tell you that's how they are here,' the old man assured the family.

Later that day, another family came by in the same way, and asked the same question. The old man again asked about their previous town, and the father replied that their town had been very unfriendly, and they had been miserable there. 'I'm sorry to tell you that's how they are here,' was the old man's reply.

It's a good story, and the conclusion is usually true.

That is not to say that a new situation will become perfect overnight, or an old environment can be left behind in a week. It took David eighteen months to feel right and at home away from his beloved North East in the new surroundings of the Midlands. 'Geordieland' is famous for its friendliness, and that was the great thing he missed, despite a major job improvement. The financial package offered was too good to miss. But where were the fun of the old office, the nearness of family, the secure environment, the familiar surroundings and the happy neighbourhood? It seemed they had been left for draughty temporary accommodation, an office full of cliques and a lonely family in an uninspiring city. What a bereavement! Like Ann and Francis, it was easy to drive back each weekend to parents who were also bereft, and David felt guilty for creating this whole situation.

Ten months is a long time to wait for your own home, and the days dragged by. Where was help, and a way out of this depression? Wives are good at finding answers, and David's wife Yvonne got to know the folk who went to a local church. She and David were impressed with their friendship and the special love the church exuded. A pub night put on by the men of the church made David feel included, and getting their own home enabled him to put down roots. After eighteen months, David felt the journey South, rather than North, was the way home. Work is getting to be much more enjoyable, and a very special thing has happened: both David and Yvonne have become Christians, largely through the love and friendship of those church folk. The bereavement is over, as new life has begun. In Jesus Christ, they have met 'a friend who sticks closer than a brother' (Proverbs 18:24).

That is something many Christians need to be reminded of, even when they move for the most noble of motives. A minister I know was heartbroken at leaving one church to move to a new one in another town after nearly twenty years which he described to me as the happiest of his life. When you have been so long as a minister that you are taking the weddings of those you once baptised, you are part of the family. When 'Quentin' went to see his doctor because he was depressed, he was told he was going through a bereavement. How he wanted to go back! In the end he drove through his old area, tears running down his face, praying out loud, 'I relinquish this place to you, Lord.' He had to deliberately leave his old life by an act of will, however hard the new life was proving. By so doing, he was able to build his new church into his, as well as God's, family. Some bereavements need a deliberate setting aside, as Quentin did. He has proved the strength of Psalm 91:1–2: 'He who dwells in the shelter of the Most High will rest in the shadow of the Almighty. I will say of the Lord, "He is my refuge and my fortress, my God, in whom I trust."'

When I saw Quentin he was just over his feelings of bereavement. When I talked with Christine, she was right in the depths of hers. Sometimes bereavement is a juggling act, and it is hard to catch each ball which goes up in the air. For Christine, she has had to face too many losses at once, and coping with each one is nearly impossible. Her husband accepted a new job with a charitable organisation, which also necessitated a move to a different part of the country. They faced the immediate prospect of leaving their elder daughter behind to complete her education. The very idea 'slayed' Christine. It was then decided that husband Brian would commute, which meant he was away from home during the working week. This went on for two years, and by the time they finally moved the elder daughter had gone to university, and the younger girl was about to embark on a career in the police force.

What a lot of changes Christine faced: a big dip in income from Brian's job; both children moving on; leaving a home they had built from nothing over nearly fifteen years; saying goodbye to a wonderful set of friends and a happy community; changing jobs from one where she felt fulfilled to another of a more ordinary nature; and coming to a city where she knew virtually no one. That is what I meant by a juggling act: for Christine there was too much to cope with all at once. She went through periods when she could not talk to anyone about the move without bursting into tears. Losing her job was especially tough, as was the farewell to their house.

Several months after the move, Christine told me she felt numb and emotionless about most things, and still full of tears. Every area of her life had been changed by the move, and the only place she felt normal was in bed with her eyes shut! When she rationalised what had happened, she realised they had their health and strength, and Brian was now in a job where he could do a great deal of good. But getting this notion from head to heart was apparently impossible, and life felt like a big black hole.

What is she going to do now? She is going to be patient, slowly recovering from the shock of it all. She is helping Brian to make their new house into a real home. And she is letting God show her that the move is right: she knows it is, but needs his reassurance. At times like this, someone like Christine needs to hear God's promise: 'Fear not . . . you are mine. When you pass through the waters, I will be with you' (Isaiah 43:1–2).

Even yelling at God is allowed in these circumstances, as my friend Fiona found out. Fiona went out to West Africa to help an organisation translating the Bible into local languages. Her move meant huge changes, with an enormous dip in income and a culture shock being the dominant problems. The latter was encapsulated in a splendid moment when she was offered a bath on arrival, to find that meant a basin in a mud hut, and a coffee mug to pour water over herself! Her real bereavement was discovered on her holiday in Britain nearly three years later, when she found her step-father had sold the family home and she was rootless. Returning to Africa, there were discomforts, but her own home there was great. She succeeded in overcoming her bereavement because she learned to live in the reality of where she was, not for ever longing for where she had been. When things got bad, as on the day she got sun-stroke on a bike ride, she would tell God, 'You brought me here, so get me out of this!'

A move like Fiona's is a reminder to all Christians that this world is not our final home, and a 'pilgrim' approach is vital: loving a home in a particular place too much only leads to hurts if a move is called for. When God called Abraham to go from one country to another in Genesis 12, Abraham got up and went, with splendid results. Fiona found that too.

It is harder when a move is forced, especially if you are taken from a good work you are doing, as Charles discovered. He had been a chaplain in the Sudan for twelve years, when he was deported by the Government in less than twelve hours. A wonderful job, a whole way of life, friends and colleagues, the happiness of an African community – all torn away in a moment. England's supermarkets, with their canned music and canned food, were

a poor substitute, and the word 'deportee' on his pass-
port meant no return to the land he loved. Where was
this oddity, back from the desert, to go?

It took several months to acclimatise, and there is still
an 'if only'. But life has gone on, and Charles now has an
excellent job which takes him all over Europe. Charles
put it well when he told me, 'There comes a time when
we have to leave and move on to the next stage of God's
plan for us, even though the process can be quite a
painful one.'

So – let's move, and aim to be happy! And if we are
looking for the best home of all, the good news comes
from Jesus: 'In my Father's house are many rooms . . . I
am going there to prepare a place for you. And . . . I will
come back and take you to be with me' (John 14:2–3).

14

No Job

Nobody likes me, everybody hates me,
I'm going down the garden to eat worms:
Long thin slimy ones, short fat fuzzy ones,
Gooey, gooey, gooey, gooey worms.

Children have some lovely rhymes! Alas, that is how many adults feel, especially those who wish they had work, but find themselves living in days of redundancies, early retirements and unemployment. Nobody seems to want you, and the loss of self-worth is a desperate bereavement. We live in a society where you are what you do, and a job gives both structure and purpose to a life. Without a job, a whole way of life is gone, and feelings of worthlessness and betrayal arise, with nothing to do. Moving from one home to another, as we considered in the last chapter, is often hard, but is usually made with a sense of purpose and progress. Having no job usually means the opposite of both these positives. How can we cope with this one?

First of all there is the dashed hope and the unkept promise, as Andrew found. As a young man heading for university, he was delighted when a major industrial concern offered to sponsor him for his engineering degree. Each summer, during the long vacation, he worked for his sponsors, glad to be saved the hassle of needing to look for work when he left university. He was aware that vacancies were limited, but at Easter the operations manager seemed keen, though there were rumours on the shop floor that all was not well. In May, the very month of his final exams, Andrew received a letter which began, 'I regret to inform you. . . .' Not one sponsored student was offered employment.

Months of frustration have followed, and no work in engineering has been forthcoming. Andrew has had to face up to his disappointment of being involved with his sponsors for so long and getting nothing in the end, having received their encouragement to be committed to them; he really did want his future to be there. No one else has anything worth while for him, and driving vans to deliver sandwiches is hardly the substitute he wanted. His mood swings from frustration to apathy, and his time is spent (when not delivering sandwiches) doing odd jobs around the house, or being fed up along with his unemployed friends. At least he is young, and willing to search for a new opening. It is a hard way for a Christian young man to learn what God encourages in Romans 12:12: 'Be joyful in hope, patient in affliction, faithful in prayer.'

While there are those who, like Andrew, have never had permanent employment, there are others, like Frances, who have deliberately left work. Surely their situation is easier? The answer is, not necessarily. Frances was a very successful pharmacist, working over a wide area of the country as an area manager responsible for sixteen pharmacies. Her husband Peter commuted long distances each day for his job, leading eventually to their moving to be near his work, and Frances leaving her position. Although she missed it, in some ways it was good to give up. She had been driven by her job, and she felt there was more to life than just work, with all the associated stress.

Eventually, Frances obtained work as a locum pharmacist, which meant a day here, a week there and no sense of belonging. After a period at one pharmacy, she left, became pregnant and now has two small children. To her surprise, this leaving work, though for the best of reasons, has caused a real bereavement. So much of who she was related to her professional position, and she now feels a loss of identity. 'I've lost "me",' she says. 'Now I'm "Peter's wife", or "Charlotte's mother", and I can't do my own thing.' If life was busy before, now she never has a moment to herself, with children who are active all day and stay awake most of the night.

Frances longs for intellectual stimulation. There is no time to concentrate on anything for more than five minutes, and her brain seems as if it is turning to jelly. She misses adult conversation which covers subjects other than babies and nappies! Life seems, at best, to be on hold. Also grieving her father's recent death, she is a long way from an extended family's help. Her self-confidence and self-worth have been at a low ebb, and life has been boring.

But life is changing for the better, slowly but surely. Frances' secret is to take each day at a time, and to place each day in God's hands, because he can keep a grip on things even when she cannot. As the children grow, there is an end in sight to their constant demands. As she lets God help her, others have commented on how she is calmer and more relaxed. Getting out to a little group run by the church, where she can read the Bible with others, has proved a way out too, even if one of the best things about it is a creche where someone else looks after the children for an hour. Survival, and a future hope, is the name of Frances' game.

There is also the knowledge that her value does not rest with what she does, but with who she is. It was Jesus who had to help his own disciples with this difficulty, as he reminded them of their eternal value, and that the very hairs on their heads were numbered (Matthew 10:30–31). It is a fact many need to take on board, and none more so than those who have no work because they have been thrown out, or, as it is euphemistically put these days, 'given early retirement' or 'made redundant'. We are special to God whatever our circumstances, not because of a special service we render.

In saying this, I have no intention of minimising the impact redundancy has on a person, and the devastation caused to many a life by it. Virginia Ironside, the famous 'Agony Aunt' with a national newspaper, was made redundant in December 1992, and though she wrote most amusingly about it, she nevertheless described it as 'horrible', and felt she needed to write a letter to herself. In talking with friends who have lost their jobs this way, every one of them has been badly hit and seriously hurt.

For some, it was the loss of income which was the worst aspect, and the effect of that was catastrophic for 'Harry' and his wife 'Tracy'. Harry's big mistake was to change jobs, though it seemed eminently sensible at the time. He had been working for a firm which had expected seven days a week from him and lots of travelling, and he was glad to get a new job nearer home, especially with a company car. When he joined, there were nearly twenty employees; eleven months later, when he got the push, there were fewer than five. With under a year's service, there was no redundancy money.

As the job went, so did both income and car. Like so many others, Harry and Tracy were living to the limit of their finances, and they crashed. They had moved into their house on the understanding that Tracy would work, but an unexpected baby meant that instead of two incomes, there was not even one. Any odd jobs Harry did meant his unemployment benefit was reduced, and the same would have happened had Tracy returned to work. Days were taken up talking with the bank and the mortgage company, who assured them all would be well and then threatened repossession of the house. In the end they had to sell, and lost thousands of pounds in the process.

With nowhere to live, the family at first rented accommodation, and subsequently moved into property owned by other family members. When I talked with them, they were in a two-bedroomed house belonging to a relative, while that relative lived with another family member, their fourth move in one summer. All their furniture was in storage. Harry said it was impossible to describe what they felt on losing the home they had taken their entire married life to build, and Tracy said she spent her whole life crying. She can hardly face other people, even at the school gates, or at church. They say that they feel they have been 'to hell and back'. In sharing this with others who know them, I know help has been offered. But Harry and Tracy are so broken that they are unable to see that help, or receive offered friendship. All they long for is a job for Harry. They are in despair, and they are not unique.

'Lizzie' feels that way about her situation too. As with some of the others with whom I have spoken, Lizzie was deep in the middle of her bereavement when I saw her, but I do not doubt that she will get through. Lizzie's redundancy was an even bigger shock than Harry's. Her loss was not so much the money but the position she held, and the enormous job satisfaction she enjoyed. She had worked for more than ten years as a senior member of staff for a major Christian organisation. Departments were being merged, but everyone was told there would be no job losses until, at the end of a day-long meeting, it was announced that three senior staff would be going. A few days later, with no interview or warning, Lizzie was handed a letter to say she was being made redundant. 'I fell apart,' she told me.

You are allowed to be angry sometimes, and she called her boss 'Judas'. How glad she was to have caring friends who came round to her flat, staying with her over that first weekend of shock. Back at work on Monday, Lizzie was determined not to give up. In those few weeks before she left she was never given any reason why she was the one to be asked to leave. She found she could leave earlier than her employers said, and took a couple of months to sit around and lick her wounds. With her redundancy money she treated herself, as a single lady, to a once-in-a-lifetime round-the-world trip for three months.

But her return home found her still bitter, and nearly a year on she had not recovered. Perhaps most sadly of all, Lizzie told me that if asked she would go back to work for those employers tomorrow. She has not been able to cut herself free from what she saw as the best job of her life. As a keen Christian, she is not sure where God is in all this, but was extremely helped by some friends who told her that she did not have to hold on to her own faith: they would hold on to it for her. People hurt for her, and she knows God has not gone away, nor does he deserve blame for what happened.

At least Lizzie knows how millions of others without work feel, especially the pain of losing all her self-confidence. I asked Lizzie how anyone in her situation can cope, and she said that she herself had found four things helpful. The first thing is to realise that when you lose a job after several years, especially if you really enjoyed it, you are in a bereavement. This will be a very part of you, and you will go through a grieving process. Lizzie included in her grief the elements of denial, numbness, shock and anger. She likened it to a bereavement through death (she had recently lost her mother), saying how it would come back and hit her when she thought she was over it.

Secondly, she found the best support was in talking to friends, again and again. As with any bereavement, this helps to sort out your feelings. Thirdly, Lizzie found someone who could help with the practicalities of redundancy, such as tax-free pay in lieu of notice, the right to work her notice, how to get her pay free of National Insurance, and so on. Finally, Lizzie needed to remember that not only did Jesus love her, but that love was not dependent on her feelings for him, and his love could be received through the practical help of others. Faithful friends held her up, and she is coming through with God's help via them.

In talking with Lizzie, I was aware of two things. In the first place, I realised I was only hearing one side of the story, and there may have been all sorts of reasons for her leaving. But, as she was never told, her story is the way people do view what happened. Secondly, how much we need God at such a time: 'If the Lord had not been on our side . . . the flood would have engulfed us, the torrent would have swept over us' (Psalm 124:1, 4).

Lizzie is not the only one struggling, but it was a relief to meet 'Philip', who has come through his grieving over his redundancies to a winning position. I put redundancy in the plural, because he had two, both of them serious. Philip was a 'whizz-kid' in industry, and rose to the top. With excellent management training, his experience took him to MD – managing director of a huge part of a nationally-known company. Those heady heights are dangerous, and, despite some excellent work, the company pushed him out when it reorganised. 'It was a desolate experience,' was how Philip described it to me. People around him found it hard to cope with 'failure', and he desperately hunted work.

Six months later, he was MD again. This time he was heading up another famous-name company's outlets – a job which meant a move across country. Five years later, he was out again. Industry uses people as it uses machinery, and a new chief executive wanted his own new team. When you scale the heights, you are proud of your position and the respect it brings from competitors and colleagues. With the sack you think all that regard has gone, and only later do you find that the respect for you as a person stays. Philip and his wife were in a strange environment after their move, and there was no work. He sat around at home doing a few odd jobs, with nowhere to go.

Too young to retire, he needed a job, and wrote round to his many contacts. While waiting for something to turn up, Philip came to two vital realisations. He needed God's help, so one day he and his wife stood in their hallway and prayed, 'OK, Lord, you're boss. We believe and trust implicitly in you.' That led, secondly, to an understanding of how he had been living; he had been a driven man, with a burden to succeed, and that was not hugely important in God's eyes. He did grieve for his job, but he let God give him peace of mind, and he was able to accept that it was wrong to be judged by his position, how much he earned and what he did. Important though they were, they were not the ultimates of life.

Philip did get other work eventually, but the greatest thing is that he has risen above the problem. He has come to see his value before God for who he is, and for the personal relationship he has with God. It is a man at peace with himself and with God who can say, as Milton did on his blindness, 'They also serve who only stand and wait.'

Redundancy does leave untidy ends, and no job to go to can mean a loss of self-value and a feeling of uselessness. But it can also give a unique opportunity to focus on our eternal worth to the God who loves us for being who we are. It's a time to look up.

15

A Handicapped Child

She ran up to me, distraught. 'There's something very wrong with the baby,' she cried, as she threw herself into my arms. My poor sister: she had waited so long for a child, and now it seemed as if it had all fallen apart.

In the next two chapters we are going to face two sorts of bereavement caused by things going wrong with body and mind. Chapter 16 will look at the huge problems for both sufferer and carer caused by a long-term illness, but here I want to consider the loss to parents of not having the perfect child they hoped for, and how those parents can cope with what is, I believe, a deep and painful bereavement. While aware of this in theory, I met it close at hand with my sister, as she awaited the birth of her first child.

Sue and Derek had been married quite a few years before they started their family. Being a health visitor, she knew all the procedures, and was pleased to hear that the probe she had at sixteen to twenty weeks showed that a normal boy was on the way. At thirty weeks, Sue went for a scan, and knew she should be allowed to see the result at once. The radiologist called in a colleague, and they pleaded that lack of time prevented Sue seeing the result. This was put in an envelope for her doctor and given to her as she left.

Being a normal, curious mother-to-be, Sue opened the report in the car, to be met with the horrifying news: 'This baby is grossly abnormal in the formation of its abdominal wall,' with possible cancer, a large hernia and all the intestines hanging out. One can only guess how she managed to drive to her health centre, where she had worked for eleven years, but when she put the report on her doctor's desk she broke down in floods of tears. Her baby had just about everything wrong with it, and would be multi-handicapped.

It was the time Billy Graham, the American evangelist, was holding a series of meetings in Sheffield. I was helping as an associate evangelist, and Sue was singing in the choir, which is how we met that evening, when she told me the news. I knew one or two of the local church leaders, and I asked a couple of them to pray with her and for her and the unborn baby, which they did. The next evening I was able to ask Cliff Barrows, the choir conductor, to pray with us, and Sue and Derek were aware of the love and prayers of many, and a sense of being amazingly surrounded by people who cared. There is no doubt that those who suffer in this way do need to feel and know the strength of caring friendship.

During the next ten weeks, Sue and Derek went through a real sense of bereavement, with the shock and grief of not expecting a normal child, and the sense of loss this brought. At the same time there was a healing through the support and prayers of others. It is at times like these that even the more undemonstrative can show their concern. At the church where he worshipped, our father went to a healing service to ask for God's help for his unborn grandchild, and found that strengthened him too in his own sorrow. My wife wrote to Sue, 'If the baby is handicapped and you can't cope, we'll take it till you're ready. And if you're never ready, don't mind.' Tokens of love like that enable the very worst to be faced.

Come the birth, Sue was induced, not knowing what would happen. As the baby was born, the consultant lowered it onto his knees, and his eyes met Sue's. 'Is it too bad?' she asked. 'No,' he replied, 'not too bad – and it's a little girl! Would you like to see her?' All Sue could see was a great mass of liver, intestines and so on hanging out, but after they had cleaned her a little they swaddled her like a normal baby, and then she saw her baby, not the problems. In seconds the baby was whisked away, and Derek hardly dared breathe in the ambulance as they dashed to the children's hospital nine miles away in nine minutes for emergency operations.

I visited them a couple of days later, as the checks went on every fifteen minutes, day and night. Tiny little babies, with tubes everywhere, entombed in incubators, are worrying sights. But a miracle did happen, and Sue and Derek have the most beautiful daughter, perfectly put back together. Her only problem is a scar where her tummy button should be, which is a remarkable nothingness compared with the prognosis at thirty weeks, and the first sight at birth. It makes our Esther a precious little lady, especially as she helped us all to understand, in a small way, the grief of many parents who want perfection in their child and do not get it.

Many stories do not have that sort of happy ending, and I have talked with a number of parents who have had to live with their bereavements long term. What has impressed me is their universal optimism and courage, and the way they live so positively with their child's problems. This is a bereavement which can, and must, see victory for the sake of the child. More than almost all the other difficulties in the whole of this book, the ones who face the enormous burdens in this chapter have worked out what to do. I discovered this as I talked with 'Gail'.

Married to 'Len', Gail felt something was wrong after only six or seven weeks of pregnancy, though she had no idea why. Marks on X-rays failed to show what was wrong, and when 'Margaret' was born, Gail was the only one not surprised when the baby was diagnosed as having spina bifida and microcephalous, which later developed into hydrocephalus. But not being surprised did not mean she was not upset. Even the doctor broke down in tears, and Len was both shocked and distressed. The consultant spelled out the implications – Margaret would be paralysed from the waist down, doubly incontinent, never walk, have possible brain damage and live only a few weeks.

Gail never blamed anyone, but she was shocked, and she went through a lot of anger with God from which she took a long time to emerge, suffering much grief and depression. Looking back, she believes that this anger was extremely important, as it enabled her to be honest, not only with God, but with herself, and she has seen others who bottled up their feelings to their own detriment. Reading the books of Job and Psalms in the Bible was good therapy; after all, Job was a good man and bad things happened to him and his family.

As Margaret has grown to be a teenager, not dying as the consultant suggested, Gail is able to see that some things are simply a mystery; God allows suffering and yet is in control, and she must give the whole situation over to him. I can write this as a theory, but Gail says it from a dozen years of experience. What she and Len have done is look for the positive things to enrich their lives, such as helping other parents of sick and disabled children come to terms with their lot. They have campaigned for children with disabilities, and have won some battles – a thing they would never have done without Margaret. They have made opportunities out of their sadness, such as pushing for better integration in education.

Has she stopped shouting at God? Yes, she has. She has come to identify with her favourite Bible person, Job, especially where God and Job talk together in chapters 38 and 42, when God says he has always been in charge, and Job admits he did not understand. Gail says she was angry because she did not understand, and she now accepts that with God's love and help they are working things out. God did answer their prayers that Margaret's back would heal, and it never crosses her mind to compare Margaret with other children. Her daughter can now read a little, draw, cook and join in with others at organisations like the Girls' Brigade. Her life is full and has quality. Of course, it does mean a lot of hard work.

Gail and Len have been helped by finding things Margaret can do. It is good to meet with other parents in similar circumstances, as they can understand the ups and downs, and the sadness. The prayer and practical help from the church has been vital, and they have felt God being close to them as a family (they now have two more children, both absolutely healthy). They need to help Margaret with her natural disappointment at not being able to do what other children can, and they are all comforted that God feels their pain, and shares it. Above all, they are not going to let evil win, as they do what Hebrews 12:15 says: 'See to it that no-one misses the grace of God and that no bitter root grows up to cause trouble.'

'No matter how handicapped Margaret is, she will be perfect in heaven,' says Gail. In the meantime, they give this life their best shot. Paul says in Romans 8:21 that creation will one day be set free from all its suffering. He admits, in verse 22, that it is 'groaning' at the moment. And many parents with a handicapped child feel this 'groaning' within themselves. Some seem to struggle more, and longer, than Gail and Len, and that was the experience of Pam and Trevor after Edward was born.

Pam was eighteen when Edward arrived, six months after their wedding, and she was told that he was perfectly healthy and normal. But as the months went by, he failed to develop as he should, and the hospital was extremely economical with the truth. Only after a year did the consultant explain that Edward had cerebral palsy, and that his progress would be slow. At nineteen, just going into her first home, Pam sought to treat him as normally as possible. What a challenge. For a year she coped, and then it dawned on her how dreadful it all was, with a child of two who could barely drag himself round the floor.

She became very depressed, and life didn't seem worth living. Both sets of parents said Edward would be all right, which was patently not the case, and Pam felt isolated. Her relationship with Trevor deteriorated and she wept as she could not face spoon-feeding a child who acted like an eight-month-old baby. Her bereavement was all too simple: she wanted the child she had wanted, not the 'thing' lying in front of her. She even tried to take an overdose, but was saved by Trevor arriving home early from work and making her sick. The doctor sent her to a psychiatrist, and help finally arrived when a new consultant for Edward took him in to hospital and sent Pam and Trevor off on holiday for a week. At the same time, the nursery arranged a meeting for parents of children with disabilities, and she found relief in talking with mums who had a similar life to hers. From then on, there were others around her, and the bereavement bottomed out.

As time went by, the family moved south, and a nursery nurse volunteered to have Edward in her Sunday school class. He was delighted, but Pam struggled. She felt God had punished her for having sex before marriage, and she could not understand why God had done this to her.

Clearly, she felt, God did not love her. At family services, she would walk out halfway through, and she continued to feel frustrated for Edward, who at ten could neither walk nor talk. One evening, before Edward and Trevor were due to go away for a few days, Pam found Edward praying in his room. 'How sweet,' she thought, 'but how can he pray to a God who has made him that way?' Then she went to a service where she had to resist her own enjoyment of the music, and the preacher challenged her to give herself to God. She told God that he was bad news, and she heard the preacher say that some people blamed God – and she knew that was her.

Pam spoke with a friend that day, and told her she wanted to know Jesus, but did not know if he wanted her because of her anger. Then she did a great thing: she forgave God for giving her Edward; and then she let God forgive her! Now Trevor is a Christian too, and they have been extremely helped by an incident in the life of Jesus, when he met a blind man. At the beginning of John 9, Jesus is asked by his disciples, 'Who sinned, this man or his parents, that he was born blind?' For Pam and Trevor it was as if Jesus' answer was for them: 'Neither this man nor his parents sinned . . . but this happened so that the work of God might be displayed in his life.'

The guilt of extra-marital sex, the anger of years, the regrets about Edward, have been healed by that loving answer. Now, they are not bothered by the 'why?' of Edward's disability and, though he cannot communicate verbally, he can and does communicate his faith. They, and many others, have had their lives enriched through Edward as he brings God's joy to them. As he grows to manhood in a residential establishment, bereavement has changed to happiness. God 'does not willingly bring affliction or grief to the children of men' (Lamentations 3:33).

This lesson always has to be learned, and the longer it takes to get there the harder it can be. But what a relief, and a release, when all the grieving is ended. I am sure one of the biggest mistakes is to bottle it all up and to suffer agonies as a result. Ann did that over Jane. Jane had an injection go wrong at ten months, and became severely handicapped as a result. Ann and her husband Roger had had their infant son die a year before Jane's birth (his part of their story is in Chapter 5), and Ann could not believe this second tragedy could happen to them. She was bitter and angry with God, blaming him that her daughter could not grow up in the way others would. She became agoraphobic and claustrophobic, and could see no purpose in living.

After many years, a friend phoned one day to invite her on a canal trip. Saying she could not go because of her claustrophobia, she broke down in tears. All her bereavements rushed into one: her mother's death, her son's death, her daughter's handicap. She cried all evening, all night and into the morning, till her husband told her at breakfast, 'Stop crying, it's bad for the children' (they had one more healthy child by then). It might have seemed an unhelpful demand, but life did change as she finally let go of her bitterness and grief.

Now Ann, together with Roger, can look on the positive side of life. There is no point comparing Jane with others, a nine-year-old in an adult body. As Roger told me, when your concern is not for GCSE and 'A' level exams, but, rather, whether your daughter will fall over, it puts life into perspective. They look at the pleasure Jane brings her friends at her college, and they are able to help others in similar situations. Ann, in particular, uses the hard road she has walked to enable her to empathise with those who are bitter and struggling. And they look forward to the day when they'll hear Jesus say,

'I am making everything new' (Revelation 21:5) – when Jane's less-than-perfect body will be changed for a perfect, eternal one.

Sometimes people will all but go under with their feelings of bereavement at having a handicapped child, as Ann did. Others will show remarkable resilience, and suffer largely because of things going wrong and because of the pressures, rather than out of grief. Such are Jenny and Pete, who have managed better than most people I know, and who have shown me how Christians can live splendidly. Their daughter Rachel is now an adult, and has spina bifida. Their sacrifices for her have been many, even to the extent of Pete turning down promotion at work to enable him to be around with Jenny. They have never been thrown by their huge problems, and their great secret is to live a day at a time, letting next year come when it does. Pete's theme is, 'One day at a time, sweet Jesus.'

There has been anger, and rightly so. Though the medical profession knew what was wrong, Pete and Jenny were not told until Rachel was two, and not given all the facts for a further three years. This protracted realisation was awful, but it did prevent feelings of grief arising. On the one hand they are not blind to the hardships they have faced – Pete jokingly says he can identify with the afflictions of Job. They have to deal with Rachel still being clingy and unwilling to be left, and their ultimate worry is for her welfare if she outlives them. But on the other hand they are like lights of hope to their many friends, as they radiate God's love. For them, the highlight of their lives came when Rachel was recently baptised as witness to her own Christian faith. Pete helped with the baptism by immersion, and it was said that Rachel's face looked as if she had been with Jesus.

God is the one who cares and understands, for what

does crucifixion do but render someone effectively quadriplegic? As William Temple put it:

'There cannot be a God of love,' men say, 'because, if there were, and he looked upon the world, his heart would break.' The church points to the cross and says, 'It did break.'

'It is God who made the world,' men say. 'It is he who should bear the load.' The church points to the cross and says, 'He did bear it.'

16

A Long Illness

Feelings of bereavement at not having the child we wanted can be mirrored by losing the person we once had. When a partner, a parent or a close friend becomes badly incapacitated, we may well feel a sense of grief at their not being the same. Equally, we may suffer a similar reaction if such a debility happens to us. We have faced this as a family with my step-mother.

When Mum died in 1966, Dad was only in his early fifties. One of our closest family friends was Ethel, who had herself been widowed some years before, and she was the friend who looked after my brother and sister the night of Mum's death. It was great when three years or so later she and Dad got married, and they have enjoyed over twenty years together. Then one day, while out visiting friends, Ethel had a stroke, followed by another later that day after she had been taken to hospital. In those few hours life changed irretrievably. For nearly three months Dad visited Ethel in hospital twice a day, and has cared for her at home since, despite two more strokes. She is hardly able to walk, and in her attempts to get around by herself she has broken arms and fingers through falling. She needs constant care in every way.

The wife of over twenty years is now a very different lady, even in her ability to communicate. Here is a real loss, and a very common one for the elderly. Perhaps that is why my father has been so accepting of what has happened, despite his obvious sorrow. He quoted to me the words of Amy Carmichael: 'In acceptance lieth peace.' He says there is no point in being resentful. His way of winning in this sad bereavement is to be positive. This is the time when you discover who are your real family and friends, and it gives those who care a chance to show it in practical ways. There are some who do the washing, or visit, or 'wife-sit', while others will write or phone.

Dad has been pleasantly surprised by one change: Ethel has drawn even closer to God, and she is most lucid in her prayers, being much more intimate with her loving heavenly Father. In talking with her, I found she is actually happy to accept her new situation. Even if it is quite unrealistic, she is looking forward to getting better, while realising she probably will not. Her main problem, she told me, is one of frustration at not being able to do as she wants. But she too has such gratitude for family and friends. I know I sound biased, but I do genuinely admire a couple who can face such adversity and still quote the words of Jesus, 'In this world you will have trouble. But take heart! I have overcome the world' (John 16:33).

The person who seems to feel the change most deeply is my younger brother Martin. He was only ten when Mum died, and Ethel has been his adoptive mother more than she has been for the others of us who had left home. Martin and Ethel had a special relationship, and her present condition has proved, he told me, 'a process of bereavement'. She cannot enter into his family's life as she did, and an intelligent conversation is now not possible. 'She is the same person, but she isn't,' is how he describes her. Worse still, it has brought home to him the brevity of life, and that one day, perhaps soon, both she and Dad will die, and how much he will miss them both.

He does say that ultimately that is good, because for the Christian, 'To live is Christ and to die is gain' (Philippians 1:21). But the slow losing of his second mother is a hurtful experience.

Facing the pain of another's suffering, and its impact on you, is one thing; to be in the never-ending illness as the sufferer yourself certainly has to be far worse. The relative or friend who watches the illness and helps the person concerned can find some respite elsewhere, but the sick person has no such lifeline. Theirs is a bereavement indeed. Such I found to be true in talking with Stuart, a fellow evangelist and a gifted musician. After a period of exhausting activity, Stuart found himself in bed with, he thought, a bad dose of influenza. After ten days, he felt he should be getting better, which he patently was not. As a fit young man, he decided to work himself back to health, especially as he had a full diary ahead of him. His plan failed, and his doctor told him to have a complete rest for two months. 'His words sounded like a death sentence,' Stuart recalls.

He was in the early stages of ME, the dreaded disease of myalgic encephalomyelitis, about which so little is understood, and which seems to be caused by a virus which will not go away, but which can hide itself and then pop up again and again. As those two months rolled into more months, and then years, Stuart faced all sorts of bereavements from this one cause. He was frustrated at not being able to work, especially in situations where others were relying on him. He agonised over his inability to control body and mind, as the illness struck, seemingly at random, in his arms, legs, head, wherever, as if the disease were on a guided tour of his body. He would be so weak he could not get up for weeks on end, or he would manage to walk a few paces and not get any further. As a formerly athletic, energetic go-getter, his was a serious loss. His mind would not allow him to construct sentences, or to concentrate.

The pressure he felt in family life hurt too. His wife and three children were stuck with a man who could do nothing with them or for them, even sitting as a zombie in a chair during Christmas lunch. Stuart felt so grieved for them, though they coped better than he could have hoped. How he longed to be the husband and father he wanted to be! Depressed and frustrated, all he could do was lie in bed. During times of slight improvement he would learn a bit of French, or totter to the local shops, but the changing seasons were felt only by a chill about the shoulders, and time passed with the shifting angle of sunlight on the bed.

How do you cope when something like this hits you? For Stuart, it has been a slow realisation that he must not, for his own and his family's sake, be resentful or bitter. His worth is not in his ability to work and 'perform', but in who he is. He quoted to me the famous comment, 'I am a human being, not a human doing.' He has stopped trying to understand it all, and accepted that there is a mystery in suffering, and that God is in there with him. As St Paul said in Philippians 3:10 about Christ, we can have 'the fellowship of sharing in his sufferings', and Stuart is learning this. He has been frustrated and angry with God, and finds no joy in suffering, but he is getting through with God's help. As I write, he is now much better, but he has learned that greatest lesson of being content whatever the circumstances.

For those of us who know long-term sufferers like Stuart, his is a cautionary tale against our underestimating how much they need our on-going constant love, prayers, support and encouragement.

ME is one type of long-term illness, and MS is another; multiple sclerosis, for which there is no known cure.

'Dan' has MS, and has gone through his own living bereavement for twenty years. With MS, the body's functions gradually fail. For Dan, it began with a blurring of the eyes and a tingling in the legs, and continued through impotence, incontinence, an inability to walk far, continuing eyesight deterioration and the need for a stick and then a wheelchair. He has to use incontinence pads, and live with the huge limitations which all of these problems have brought.

How do you face not being able to work full time; not being able to make love with your wife, or hike with your children, or control your bladder; or walking like an old man while you are only in your thirties or forties? Dan recommends a blend of four things: determination, confidence, accepting the state of your condition and knowing that God loves you. His lifelines of help come from a tremendously supportive wife, with whom he can share everything; from a Christian doctor with whom he can talk; and from excellent Christian friends who, though not knowing every one of the facts, pray for him and encourage him.

Like others who bear heavy loads, Dan is one who has got to the stage where he can say, 'I have learned the secret of being content in any and every situation' (Philippians 4:12), largely because God enables him to live each day as it comes. He quoted to me the words of Jesus, 'Do not worry about tomorrow . . . each day has enough trouble of its own' (Matthew 6:34). He knows the future is bleak, and faces with no joy being permanently in a wheelchair and living in a nursing home. But he is determined to keep going, to accept change, to delight in his wife's help and to trust God. I found it remarkable to hear Dan say that he counts his blessings, but I know he does. By so doing he can help others who suffer, and know God's love, whatever happens. That's how to face a living bereavement!

But let me return to those who have to stand by as others fade away before their eyes. Among them are those whose relatives suffer from Alzheimer's disease. Catherine's father took early retirement, after seeming to struggle with excessive pressure at work. Her mother and she noticed he was starting to forget things, and finding ordinary tasks harder to accomplish. He would make more mistakes when playing the organ at church, and take all day to count the church collection, compared with half an hour previously. It took two years to convince him there was a problem and he needed to see his doctor. After a prostate operation he became completely disorientated, unable to follow simple instructions to aid recovery, and he was finally diagnosed as having Alzheimer's disease.

When he was told, he did not understand, and Catherine and her mother realised the hopelessness of the situation. They were distressed as they read literature about the disease, but they had to prepare for eventualities. Her dad found it grievous to give up the organ he had played for fifty years, and not to drive any more. The next four years saw further regression, and Catherine found herself feeling guilty: guilty at being so far from the family home and not able to help, and guilty at her irritation, and the desire that he would not live long. She came to terms with the latter, not wanting her dad to lose his dignity, mentally or physically. In the end, his quality of life was reduced to zero, and he would go for periods of care in hospital to give the family a brief respite.

The bereavement caused by Alzheimer's disease is simple: the person you once knew gradually disappears and never comes back. The husband and father was, Catherine told me, to all intents and purposes, dead. In his last year, she and Mum would talk of their memories, and of what they used to do, as if he had died already. Slowly he went back to being a baby in every way, except in making progress. Death was an overwhelming relief, and Catherine felt anger that anyone should have to end their life like that. Only the first few days after he died were dreadful, and after that it was easier to talk of all the good things they remembered of this lovely man. The empty chair could be faced better now, since Mum had lived as if she were a widow for two or three years, and Catherine similarly without her dad. Within less than a year after his death, their grieving was over, and even anniversaries proved easier the year after his death than the year before.

Catherine is an agnostic, and gained her support from good friends, especially those who had experienced similar circumstances. She valued their offering of care. She was glad her mum and dad had a deep faith in God, and saw how that comforted them both. Because Alzheimer's disease is slow, there does need to be support from somewhere. The partner, especially, needs those who will befriend and sit in while they get a brief respite. The grief is to see their loved one slowly disappear, until they cannot grasp the meaning of any but the simplest sentences. The partner is isolated, and the most precious anniversaries and moments become meaningless. It is impossible to know how the sufferer feels, but the carer is grieving constantly.

A friend, whose wife has Alzheimer's disease, told me that being her husband makes it easier to give her the intimate help she needs. However, it is hard to face the change of personality in one he has loved for more than sixty years. His wife is, he says, at one and the same time both the same, and yet a different person. He manages by having his wife cared for in hospital part of the time, and by their going on holiday with friends, who can share the work. Relatives give him a break too, and others cook meals for them. This particular man has held a very high position in our country, and is most learned. Yet now he is so glad to have God's help more than anything else in his life. It was Augustine who said, 'I have read in Plato and Cicero sayings that are very wise and very beautiful; but I never read in either of them, "Come to me, all you who are weary and burdened, and I will give you rest."' Such are the words of Jesus in Matthew 11:28, and they are for those who identify with the last couple of pages.

Younger folk sometimes have to cope with the bereavement of a lingering death too, as my Uncle Ray did when my Aunt Janet was dying of cancer. My sailor uncle came home from one of his tours at sea as a chief engineer to find his young wife ill in bed, and their son with grandparents. The diagnosis began with bronchitis and ended with Hodgkin's disease, and she was transferred to a hospital for this cancer. Ray's own doctor told him on the phone she would be dead in six months, and he broke down in tears. However, the hospital gave her five years, and they were exactly right. She died at thirty-four.

In those five years Ray was bereaved throughout. To add to his burden, the doctors advised that Janet would best be occupied by having another baby, knowing she would not live to bring it up. Their four-pounds-at-birth daughter was three when Janet died. Part of Ray's bereavement was having to leave the sea, which he loved, to get a job on land to be near his dying wife. He lived the lie that Janet should not know what was happening, and wept in secret. He told me that she was never again the same woman as she had been before those last five years. She was four stone when she died, and all that time Ray had to bring up his small children, facing daily the fact that they would have no mother. Five years is a long time to grieve, and the end does not bring the consolation that the one who died was old, and thus ready to go. He had to comfort his grieving son and his wife's mother, whose husband had also recently died.

How did he survive? Part of the answer was that he found somewhere to do his grieving. Two or three times he went over the fence at the bottom of the garden into the school playing field in the middle of the night and yelled at God. Why did Janet have to die? Why were two young children left without a mother? He was not kindly disposed towards God, and thought he was cruel. Within three years he lost his wife, his sister (my mother), his father-in-law and his mother. No wonder he was angry and bitter. Even after getting over these bereavements, his anger with God remained, though he later found happiness when he married Betty, and was able to forgive God. He says now that time does heal, and God did hear his yelling. Though he did not realise it then, God helped him, and, as he has latterly become a Christian, he is at peace in himself. But it was a long, hard bereavement, and highlights the pressures people are under.

What are we to make of all this? The one with the long-term illness can try to make a positive reinvestment in their future. The next holiday could be planned, for example, and no one need say, 'I won't make it.' Let's make the best of life, and concentrate on what we can do, rather than being frustrated by what is impossible.

The caring relative will find that having a regular break to look forward to, and a day off each week, can lighten the burden. And we carers might like to be a little bit naughty, and use the problem as an excuse to stop doing some things we don't enjoy anyway!

Let's not any of us look back. Instead we can concentrate on the future, and make the best of the life we have.

In all these situations, I would want to give God the chance to enter into my need and loss with his strength and love.

PART THREE

The Way Out

The Way Out

Bereavement is to have taken from us, as if by force, anyone or anything precious in our lives – often by death itself. If we are to survive the experience then it is helpful to learn the principal features of bereavement. Unfortunately they do not come in a neat and tidy order and everyone's experience will be different. The grieving process may be very short for some, and may last a long, long time for others.

Research has shown, however, that grief does follow a pattern which is common to most kinds of loss. My own experience, and that of those with whom I have spoken, would agree with that research, and it may be helpful to set out here the main features that characterise loss of any kind.

Shock

A knock on the door, a telephone call, and our whole world can be turned upside down in a moment. The daily routine is halted, and the realisation hits us that things will never be quite the same again.

Shock can feel like a physical blow. It can cause an initial numbness that, in the early days at least, can act as a protective shell which enables us to cope with hospitals, undertakers, relatives and funerals. We may feel that we are separated from the real life going on around us, and operating only on a mechanical level, like robots.

Tears at this stage can be very therapeutic. Emotions need to be released, and I have personally found it a great relief not to bottle up my feelings – the stiff upper lip is no help.

Denial

'I don't believe it!' I cried, when my father phoned to say that my mother had died. Such a reaction is often part of the original shock and usually lasts for only a short time. But if we continue to deny that the loss has happened, if we try to leave a child's bedroom as it was when the child was alive, or if a husband continues to set a place at the table for his dead wife, then something specific needs to be done to enable this stage to be worked through. It may be helpful to view the body in the Chapel of Rest, to hold the dead baby for a while, to talk to carers about the last moments when the loved one was alive. If there is no body, then this denial stage can be complicated.

In the case of miscarriage, or abortion, giving the child a name can help us to focus our love and regret, and to accept that he or she has come – and gone.

Grief

If a bereavement is particularly hard, such as a very un-expected death, a suicide, or the end of an extremely close relationship, grief can feel like a bad illness. We are affected in every way – body, mind and spirit – and it may be that we shall need medical help if our grief leads to extremes, such as the excessive use of alcohol or drugs, or a bout of severe depression.

There may be total refusal to make any sort of new life, or a complete withdrawal from everything and everyone, and in that case we may need to seek counsel. But it is equally important that we don't try to prevent our feelings of grief. Such a denial can only bring other problems.

Growing awareness

This stage lasts longer and encompasses a variety of feelings, thoughts and physical symptoms. For most people, the first year is the worst, as anniversaries, birthdays and Christmas have to be endured. This applies equally to loss by death and to divorce, a move, or a child leaving home. The well-worn phrase 'time heals' does however hold true, particularly for the first acute and intense pain of grief.

At various times during this stage emotions will need to be worked through, and it is as well to be prepared for them.

Guilt

Self-reproach and feelings of guilt are often felt. We feel we should have done something to prevent the tragedy ('If only I'd got her to fasten her seat-belt . . .'); or we feel we did not do enough ('I should have visited more . . .'). There is a sense of failure ('I could have been a better parent . . .'); and we may wish that relationships had worked out better ('Why did we quarrel so much?').

Children especially tend to feel a sense of guilt after trauma. They do not understand why someone has died, or why their parents have divorced, and they often begin to wonder if something that they have done or said has caused the tragedy. They need to be encouraged to talk, and to be assured constantly that they are not to blame.

Anger

We will find at times that we feel anger against others – the medical services, family, friends, the church, God. 'It was the doctor's fault.' 'The vicar never visited.' 'How can I believe in a God who lets this happen?' But sometimes the most difficult feeling to understand and accept is anger towards a deceased person for dying and so leaving us deserted. We need to be real about our anger, to express it to someone who will understand, and then to learn how we can deal with it.

Depression

I have often found an 'if only' feeling at this stage. There is a yearning for who or what has been lost, a tendency to go over and over details of the days before the loss, a physical longing, extending to the sexual if that was part of the lost relationship, and a desire to visit old, familiar places. We may feel anxious and insecure. We do not know how we will cope with the future, or survive without this person, or that relationship, or that place.

Where death is involved we may have a sharpened sense of our own mortality, become concerned about dying, or even contemplate suicide.

Depression is a very common feature of bereavement, and can follow redundancy, miscarriage, divorce. Physically there may be changes in appetite and sleep patterns, tightness in the chest and throat, breathlessness, fatigue and a dry mouth. We may find it hard to function normally because of absentmindedness, restlessness and distressing dreams. When I have felt like this I have been tempted to withdraw from the help of others, endangering our friendship in the process.

Acceptance

Gradually, however, better days come. After long suffering ends for a terminally ill person, or a horrific injury or
handicap, it is fully understandable for there to come a
sense of relief. In these circumstances some people have
almost completed their grieving by the time of the
funeral and are so able to move on quite quickly.

Now there is a period of reinvestment, as life comes
together again in a new and adjusted world. It is like
spring after a long, hard winter. We might begin to find
ourselves becoming excited again about life's possibili-
ties, and to understand that after 'a time to weep' will
come 'a time to laugh'; after 'a time to mourn' there will
follow eventually 'a time to dance' (Ecclesiastes 3:4).

And there comes too the relief of knowing that we do
not have to face our problems alone. We can look around
us and find others who are willing and waiting to help.

Accepting help

Friends, Christian ministers, family are all there. Let's
recognise that they care, let's accept their help and
not push them away. We need not be ashamed to cry in
front of them. We might also want to receive counselling
from a church leader or, perhaps in special circumstances, from one of the organisations mentioned in the
Appendix.

We must understand too, though, that there will be
those who feel they should be there for us, but who are
unable to help. They may feel a sense of inadequacy
which causes them to avoid us, for fear of saying the
wrong thing.

Sometimes the greatest comfort comes from the
people who, without words, offer practical, homely com-

fort at a time when all seems bleak. The cup of tea, the cooked meal, the hot water bottle – nothing in themselves, but they can become beacons of light and love in our dark moments.

Now too is the time to understand the truth that God himself loves and cares for us. When Jesus hung on the cross, 'He took up our infirmities and carried our sorrows' (Isaiah 53:4). He loved us then; we must let him love us now. We can cry to him and with him and discover his comfort. We can ask him 'Why?' We may not be able to accept his answer straight away, but if we are willing to trust to his timing we will discover the comfort that David knew when he wrote: 'Even though I walk through the valley of the shadow of death, I will fear no evil, for you are with me' (Psalm 23:4).

The Bible tells us that Jesus himself grieved. He understands our own hurts. When his cousin John the Baptist was murdered he went off alone (Matthew 14:13), and he wept at the graveside of his friend Lazarus (John 11:35). Now he says to us, 'Never will I leave you; never will I forsake you' (Hebrews 13:5). We can find forgiveness for anything we have done wrong, and healing for our hurts. We need not stay broken. 'I am the Lord who heals you' (Exodus 15:26).

God is the ultimate judge, and we may safely leave the destiny of others to his love. We don't need to carry the burden. Rather, let's allow God to pick us up and help us to live again. 'Those who hope in the Lord will renew their strength. They will soar on wings like eagles; they will run and not grow weary, they will walk and not be faint' (Isaiah 40:31).

Letting go

This is perhaps the hardest and cruellest step of all. We

have to let our loved one, or place, or object become part of our past. The inevitability of death has to be accepted. We have to release the one who has died and leave them with God, however grievous the death – such as when a child has died. We have to let go of our might-have-beens, as with miscarriage or infertility. And we have to release the person who has wronged us, maybe in divorce or rape.

We must face the truth that the person who has died has gone and is not hovering around us as a disembodied spirit close at hand. We must never yield to the temptation of attempting to contact them. God specifically forbids this in Deuteronomy 18:11. People who have died do not come back. They go on – as Jesus said to the dying thief on the cross, 'Today you will be with me in paradise' (Luke 23:43). When we write RIP on a tombstone we mean may he or she rest in peace. Let them.

If deep matters remain unresolved between us and a deceased person, we could try the 'Gestalt Empty Chair' technique I mentioned in Chapter 6. If the problem is with someone still alive, we must learn to forgive ourselves for our failures – and forgive the other person too. It might be helpful to pray the Lord's prayer, emphasising particularly the words, 'As we forgive those who trespass against us.' It may be a parent we need to forgive, a divorced partner, people who forced us to move or lose a job, or someone who has injured us. A rape victim will need to forgive the rapist. Only in this way can we ourselves find forgiveness and peace of mind.

We should never forget the good memories that we have that can inspire and encourage us, but we must begin to look forward. This is especially important with a lost job, a broken marriage or a child leaving home. We must not ruin our prospect of future happiness by dwelling on the past. We need to believe in our future

and in who we are. We need to look for what we can do,
ignoring the can't-be-done, especially if we live with limitations, handicap or illness.

I asked my counsellor sister, Sue, if there is a moment
when she knows a person has turned this corner from the
negative to the positive. She said it comes when the
bereaved person answers the question 'How are you?' by
replying, 'And how are *you*?' When we start to be concerned for the people helping us, we are moving in the
right direction.

Helping others

Finding something positive to do will prove therapeutic,
even if our own pain is not immediately erased. Perhaps
there is a task that used always to be done by the person
who has died. Doing it yourself can bring a sense of oneness with them, and a new love for those who are left.
Given time, perhaps our hard times can help someone
cope with a similar hurt. There are great opportunities
for service, and your local church, hospital or volunteer
service will all advise you on how you can become
involved.

Those of us who are Christians will want to pray for
others who are hurting. They may feel far away from God,
or even that they have lost their faith: we can hold their
faith for them. We need to be aware of the stages
described in the last few pages. We should never force
ourselves, or presume that we are needed. Words may be
less valuable than providing a listening ear, or a shoulder
to cry on. Practical help is good – making a room available, taking children out, giving a hug (or not, depend-
ing on their needs and who we are!). People need reassurance – they don't want to be told to pull themselves
together.

Now is the time to reinvest in your family and friends. The hours that were taken up with the bereaved situation can now be filled with new and different relationships. We need to look outwards and upwards for hope and new opportunities:

Two men gazed through prison bars;
One saw mud, the other stars.

Children and bereavement

Often in traumatic situations we have a tendency to bundle children out of the way, to protect them from the reality of the situation and to shield them from a too-violent confrontation with death itself. But as we have seen in some of the stories in this book, this can lead to a life-time of regret for the child who never had the chance to say goodbye to someone important in his or her life. Sometimes a child can gain great comfort from attending the funeral, seeing others face loss, being part of the family as they learn to do without one member.

In the case of the death of a pet – and often it will be a pet that particularly belonged to a child – it may help to hold a little funeral service of your own. They can learn there that it is all right to cry, to grieve for what has gone.

Children copy what they see around them: if we deny the reality of what has happened, then so will they. They need to be allowed to talk things through, to face their own feelings of guilt, as we have seen, and to understand that the person who has gone has not become an unmentionable bogey – but is a loved memory.

Often the need to comfort and cuddle a weeping child will be the catalyst for our own tears and grief – we can help each other.

Those of us who are Christians will especially look

forward to that day when 'God will wipe away every tear' (Revelation 7:17); when 'there will be no more death or mourning or crying or pain, for the old order of things has passed away' (Revelation 21:4). If you do not yet know the joy of looking forward in this way, come on in, there is room for you! 'Come to me, all you who are weary and burdened,' says Jesus, 'and I will give you rest' (Matthew 11:28).

Bereavement is the toughest battle any of us face. Let's resolve right now that by the love of God we will be winners – and go for it.

Appendix

If you need further help, here are some organisations which may be able to give it. Try your own church minister, or a trained counsellor. The following are available at the time of writing this book. Look for one which seems to cover your need.

Each section is in alphabetical order.

SPECIFIC HELP

Association for Spina Bifida and Hydrocephalus
42 Park Road
Peterborough
PE1 2UQ
0733 555988

Help for parents encountering these problems from before birth onwards.

Alzheimer's Disease Society
Gordon House
10 Greencoat Place
London
SW1P 1PH
071 306 0606

BACUP
(British Association of Cancer United Patients) — Those with cancer, and their relatives.
3 Bath Place
Rivington Street
London
EC2A 3JR
Helpline: (Free) 0800 181199
Counselling: 071 696 9000

The Compassionate Friends — A nationwide self-help organisation of parents whose child of any age (including adult) has died from any cause: befriending not counselling.
53 North Street
Bristol
BS3 1EN
0272 539639

Contact a Family — Support for families who care for children with special needs.
16 Strutton Road
Victoria
London
SW1P 2HP
071 222 2695

Cot Death Research — Support for newly-bereaved parents.
8a Alexandra Parade
Weston-super-Mare
Avon
BS23 1QT
0836 219010

Disabled Living Foundation
380–384 Harrow Road
London
W9 2HU
071 289 6111

Equipment for all forms of
disability for children
and adults.

ME Association
4A Corringham Road
Stanford-le-hope
Essex
SS17 0AH
0375 642466

New Beginnings
20 Stratford House
Sackville Street
Southsea
PO5 4BX
0705 730250

Counselling survivors of
child abuse. Support for
families.

Rape Crisis Centre
PO Box 69
London
WC1X 9NJ
071 837 1600

Female counsellors
(24-hour service).

Relate National Marriage
    Guidance
Herbert Gray College
Little Church Street
Rugby
Warks
CV21 3AP
0788 573241

See local phone directory
for nearest branch under
Relate or NMG.

SANDS
Stillbirth and Neonatal
    Death Society
28 Portland Place
London
W1N 3DE
071 436 5881

Offers support through
self-help groups, and
befriending for parents
bereaved through
pregnancy loss and still-
birth or neonatal death.

NATIONAL HELP ORGANISATIONS

CRUSE
126 Sheen Road
Richmond
Surrey
TW9 1UR
Office: 081 940 4818
Helpline: 081 332 7227 (Weekdays, 9am–5pm)

Care for anyone who has
been bereaved by any sort
of death, plus resources
on bereavement.

Samaritans
10 The Grove
Slough
Berks
SL1 1QP
0753 532713

Confidential emotional
support by befriending
(24-hour service).
See your local phone
directory.

Westminster Pastoral
    Foundation
23 Kensington Square
London
W8 5HN
071 937 6956

Counselling for people
with emotional or
relationship problems.
(fees negotiable).

REGIONAL HELP ORGANISATIONS

The Armagh Pastoral Centre
35 Charlemont Gardens
Armagh
N Ireland
BT61 9BB
0861 525282

N. Ireland and N. Eire:
Christian counselling on
all subjects, and courses
on bereavement.

Barnabas House Christian
  Centre
Old St Clears Road
Camarthen
Dyfed
SA31 3HH
0267 230428

Care, counsel and
residential support for
those bereaved in any way,
or for those in crisis.

The Bud Christian Trust
22 Hill Street
Corbridge
Northumberland
NE45 5AA
0434 633429

Counselling on all
subjects, including
bereavement,
plus training.

Cardiff Concern
Regal House
Gelligaer Lane
Cathays
Cardiff
CF4 3JS
0222 664410

Christian counselling on
all subjects, including
bereavement.

Careline   Christian counselling for
St John's Church   all types of bereavement.
St James Road
Shirley
Southampton
SO1 5FB
0703 702122

Christian Care   Cambridge area: Christian
Old School   counselling for any
61 St Barnabas Road   significant loss.
Cambridge
CB1 2BX
0223 68264

Crossline Christian Centre   South West England:
5 Heavitree Road   24-hour counselling service
Exeter   and home visits.
EX1 2LD
0392 433333

Doncaster Canaan Trust   Pastoral care and
Hexthorpe Manor House   counselling.
Doncaster
DN4 0HY
0302 851214

Help in Bereavement   Practical support, advice
72 Wood Street   and counselling to people
Kidderminster   in bereavement.
Worcs
DY11 6UB
0562 515848

The Light House
11 Belvedere Road
Earlsdon
Coventry
CV5 6PF
0203 673734

Christian care ministry:
counselling for all types
of needs.

The Manna House
St Giles Street
Northampton
NN1 1JW
0604 22666

Counselling on all subjects
including bereavement,
plus training.

Network Christian
   Counselling
10 Cotham Park
Bristol
BS6 6BU
0272 420066

Christian counselling on
all subjects.

Oxford Christian Institute
   for Counselling
11 Norham Gardens
Oxford
OX2 6PS
0865 58154

Counselling on all subjects
(over age of 16)

REACH Merseyside
85a Allerton Road
Liverpool
L18 2DA
051 737 2121

Meeting people at their
point of need; counselling,
training and care.

Sevenoaks Christian
   Counselling Service
42 Lime Tree Walk
Sevenoaks
Kent
TN13 1YH
0732 450118

General counselling
facility from a Christian
standpoint through
professionally qualified
counsellors.

Simpson House
52 Queen Street
Edinburgh
EH2 3NS
031 225 6028

E. Scotland area:
counselling service on all
subjects.

Stockport Counselling
   Service
45 Knowsley Crescent
Offerton
Stockport
SK1 4JP
061 480 0153

Non-directive service in
all aspects of counselling.

Tom Allen Centre
32 Elmbank Street
Glasgow
G2 4PD
041 221 1535

W. Scotland area:
counselling service on all
subjects.

The Vine Christian
   Counselling Service
1582 Pershore Road
Stirchley
Birmingham
B30 2NH
021 458 2752

Personal counselling on
all forms of bereavement.